'BIG TALK' M
AT BIRCHEN C

Compiled by

Retired Chief Superintendent

BRIAN HUMPHREYS

CONTENTS

Introduction and Acknowledgements

This book is not intended to be a 'Murder Mystery' novel. It is said that most murders are committed by someone known to their victim and this murder was no exception.

This is a true story. Apart from the odd supposition which would be corroborated with circumstantial evidence or other events, nothing fictitious will be added. It will, so far as is possible, contain nothing but the true facts as was unearthed during the investigation.

What will make it interesting are the circumstances and people involved. You might ask, "How could an only child, a daughter who was besotted by her father, plan to murder him or assist in his murder?" Her meeting up with Douglas Iorworth William Ellis Casey Latham, a Walter Mitty character if ever there was one, was a cruel accident which led to disaster for both of them.

Indeed, Latham's name with five Christian names as provided by him when arrested, ought to immediately sound alarm bells. His birth was registered as Douglas I.W.E. CASEY. No sign of the surname LATHAM, but, of course, anyone is entitled to change or add to their name, as he has appeared to have done prior to the murder. Indeed, it appears that he has yet again amended his name since his release from prison.

His birth was registered as occurring in Paddington, London, during the third quarter of 1953, with his mother's maiden name registered as 'CLANFORD'. He subsequently provided his birth date as 10th August 1953. Although this date is not in dispute, it has been discovered that any facts proffered by him really require corroboration where necessary.

It is believed that he spent his early childhood in London. When he was about 12, he moved to Stourport-on-Severn, to be raised with his grandparents. It is this Stourport and Kidderminster area in Worcestershire where that dreadful mix of characters combined to sadly end in the brutal death of his girlfriend's father, Arthur John Davies. Arthur's daughter, Caroline Beatrice Davies, had tragically met up with Latham and together, they were to play out the roles of an unbelievable conspiracy, drawing in others of their like-minded friends who were all living in some fantasy world where everything they desired was to end in reality, as if by the waving of a magic wand, and with very little real effort committed by themselves.

Doug and Carol, as they were known, commenced a liaison in about September 1980 and Latham moved into the family home in October of that year. It was about 15 months later that the murder was committed. Ironically, their coming together was much against Caroline's father's wishes but Latham had soon managed to 'weasel' his way into charming the pants off Caroline. Despite her father's express wishes, they soon built a sexual relationship together at the family's home, 9 Clifton Road, on the Birchen Coppice Estate in Kidderminster.

The author, Brian Humphreys, commenced his police career as a police cadet in 1960. He joined the Herefordshire Constabulary straight from school. With other forces, this Constabulary merged to form the West Mercia Constabulary at its inception in 1967. He had worked in many of the force's towns and cities but never at Kidderminster, other than during his responsibilities on a 'force-wide' basis during periods of commanding Traffic, Operations and Criminal Investigations. He trained as a 'Hostage Negotiator' and, following his eventual promotion to Chief Superintendent, performed a two-year secondment to the Home Office as a staff officer to Her Majesty's Inspector of Constabulary, Sir John Woodcock.

Insofar as 'Criminal Investigations' were concerned, he had been a Detective Sergeant, Detective Chief Inspector in two Divisions and latterly, at the time of this murder investigation, a Detective Superintendent - one of the deputies to the head of the force's Criminal Investigation Department, Detective Chief Superintendent David Cole.

Kidderminster, or, as it is more popularly referred to, 'Kiddie' or 'Kidder', had only featured in his portfolio of places served prior to this murder, when passing through it en route to other stations in the north of the force area in Worcestershire and Shropshire. He had also investigated complaints made by members of the public against police officers stationed there. This resulted in him knowing the police station as well as any other in the force, especially, with his love of food, where the canteen was.

Kidderminster's visitors are now attracted there when visiting the West Midlands Safari Park or the Severn Valley Railway, both attractions being on the periphery of the town.

As an aside, Kidderminster will also be remembered back in 2001 when Richard Thomas Taylor stood for Parliament as an 'Independent Kidderminster Hospital and Health Concern' candidate. He had been a member of his local health authority, chairman of Kidderminster Hospital League of Friends and a committee member of the 'Save Kidderminster Hospital' campaign, which ran from 1997 until 2001.

His main issue was the restoration of the hospital's 'Accident and Emergency' department which, due to cuts to the NHS budget, had been closed a year earlier.

Having ousted the incumbent Labour MP with an 18,000 majority, he was re-elected in 2005, making him the first Independent MP to retain his seat since 1979. He was eventually defeated in the 2010 General Election by a Conservative candidate.

Like most towns, it has those areas within it which are occupied by those more inclined towards criminality. There are quite large areas of houses owned by the Local Authority and occupied by many who need to be supported by the 'Benefits System'. Many of these houses have been purchased by their occupants from the Kidderminster Borough Council, which then became part of the Wyre Forest District Council. It was such an estate, Birchen Coppice, where, on 27th January 1981 at 9 Clifton Road, Arthur John Davies was cruelly bludgeoned to death.

As head of the force's 'Criminal Investigation Department, Detective Chief Superintendent David Cole headed the investigation and it was he who delegated the author, Detective Superintendent Brian Humphreys to lead the 'on the ground investigation' when it came to interviewing the prime suspects. He was very ably assisted by Detective Chief Inspector Ian Bullock and Detective Inspector Peter Herbert. He very much wishes to acknowledge their tremendous assistance in this endeavour.

Not long prior to the commission of this murder, the lessons learned from the Peter Sutcliffe, 'Yorkshire Ripper' murders had resulted in a computerised system concerning evidence gathering and the compilation and management of tasks to be performed. This was called 'HOLMES', an acronym for 'Home Office Large Major Enquiry System'. It was rapidly installed at the police station and operated by those specially trained for the purpose.

Other than the deceased, the main 'players' in the case included his daughter, her boyfriend and all of their implicated friends, whether suspects or witnesses. Many of them were characters who more often than not, frequented The Bridge Inn, Mill Street, Kidderminster. Some, including the main suspects, possessed grandiose ideas, but lacked the ability to turn their dreams into reality without resorting to criminality.

Such were the twists and turns of their plans and actions to dispose of Mr Davies, which first grew from loose and unbelievable 'Big Talk' but which transpired and ended with the taking of his life, that Brian Humphreys swore that someday, he would write a book about it. To that end, he was permitted to retain his 'working copy' of the report published for the information of the Director of Public Prosecutions, whose authority and guidance was required to proceed with the relevant charges preferred against the defendants.

So, after 41 years, here is that book, with an apology to the late Assistant Chief Constable, Mr Alan Vickers, for not promptly returning the file which he discovered in a plastic box in his loft at the time of moving home, many years later.

Acknowledgements

Any reader will quickly appreciate that among many others, the two main support pillars Brian Humphreys relied upon during the many protracted interviews undertaken with suspects, were Detective Chief Inspector Ian Bullock, the then DCI of the Telford Division and Detective Inspector Peter Herbert of the Kidderminster Division. Peter also tied up all loose ends of the investigation prior to submitting the final report to the Director of Public Prosecutions department. There were, of course many others, too many to name.

Retired DCI's Barrington (Barrie) Mayne and DCI Keith Smith also came to our aid particularly with the arrests of McLaughlin and Breakwell. Barrie retired as Detective Chief Superintendent and Keith as a Superintendent.

He also wishes to thank others who have volunteered to proof read the book in particular, his friend, retired solicitor, David Hallmark for persuading Barney Burnham to cast his professional eye over it. Barney is an author in his own right and now a retired journalist and broadcaster.

In addition, his golfing mates, Dr. Rick Wilkinson and Jim Jackson have also contributed much to the content and through their proof reads, were also able to suggest many corrections and amendments.

1. - First Steps

The Headquarters of the Force's Criminal Investigation Department was at Hindlip Hall, Worcester where, in addition to Scenes of Crime personnel and other forensic and clerical departments, the Head of the Force CID, Detective Chief Superintendent David Cole sat together with his deputy, a Detective Superintendent, (then myself) and a Detective Chief Inspector, Alan Poulton.

I had been appointed as a Detective Superintendent on 24th November 1980 to replace Alan Mayo, who was unfortunately absent on long term sick leave. I had been a Detective Chief Inspector, first at Malvern and then at Worcester, before being promoted to Superintendent in the Force Operations Department, which was also located within force headquarters.

I suspect therefore that my selection to fill Alan's gap was not as a result of my 'Sherlock' abilities, but as a matter of convenience in that I was an ex-senior detective and very handily placed, just a few offices away from the headquarters CID offices.

The 27th January 1981 was no different from any other Tuesday except that during the morning the three of us mentioned above plus two other Divisional Detective Chief Inspectors met in the office to discuss the ongoing case of the disappearance of a vulnerable young lady who we presumed was then deceased. It was later that day when DCI Poulton and I were together in my vehicle when we received information, I think through one of our pagers, to attend the scene of a body found under suspicious circumstances at 9 Clifton Road, Kidderminster.

We raced towards Kidderminster but it must be remembered that in those days, we had no mobile phones for general issue and the lack of digitised systems meant that we were without satellite navigation. With neither of us having the necessary local knowledge, this meant that when we neared the area of what we thought was the Birchen Coppice Estate, we needed to enquire of the public as to the directions we required.

We soon found the address, arriving there at around 5pm. Local Police vehicles and the ambulance service had arrived before us, which made the area well-lit with blue flashing lights. Being located among many other houses on quite a large council housing estate meant that the grim discovery had soon generated quite a flurry of activity.

My friend to this day, Superintendent Phil Langford, the commander of the Kidderminster Division, was there. Between us, we tried to command calm among all those anxious to help and offer information. It is usually the case at such incidents when they break, that people are anxious to be involved, but often have nothing to contribute when their contribution is finally analysed.

The first item on the agenda was to protect the scene and preserve evidence. I quickly learned that it was Mrs Betty Davies, wife of the deceased, who discovered her husband's body on returning home from work, just over an hour before we reached the scene. In addition, two ambulance operatives and two police officers had already viewed the body as it lay in situ. They were followed by Detective Inspector Herbert and a Detective Sergeant Griffiths from the Kidderminster CID.

With seven people already having entered the house, viewed the body and ascertained that no other person was on the premises, there was no reason which required myself or DCI Poulton to follow them. Arrangements were therefore put into place to seal the house until the arrival of personnel connected with the examination of the scene and body and evidence-gathering requirements. In that context, Detective Chief Superintendent Cole, together with 'Scenes of Crime' officers, arrived approximately 10 minutes after us.

They were followed by Dr. Weston of the West Midlands Forensic Science Laboratory and later by Dr Norman Gower, a Home Office Pathologist.

Following a preliminary inspection of Mr Davies' body at the scene, it was conveyed to the Kidderminster Mortuary where, during that same evening, Dr Gower performed a post-mortem examination. In his opinion, death would have occurred very rapidly after injuries were inflicted and unconsciousness would have been virtually instantaneous, after the first of three blows to the head by a heavy, narrow or edged metal weapon.

It was thirteen days later, when Dr. Gower examined a straight length of wheel brace and concluded that this tool could have caused the head and facial injuries suffered by Mr. Davies.

However, returning to the first activities at the scene, a large Sherpa Police Bus had arrived in which I gathered the police officers together for a brief conference so as to learn what, if anything, of significance had occurred prior to our arrival. In addition to knowing that the deceased's wife, Betty Davies, had discovered her husband's body, I also learned that his daughter, Caroline Beatrice Davies and her boyfriend, Douglas Latham, who also lived at the premises, had arrived at their house about twenty-five minutes before we had arrived.

Police Sergeant Jones had informed them of Mr. Davies's death and they joined the melee, which of course, involved the tragic death of Caroline's father. With Latham having five Christian names, he was mostly referred to as 'Douglas' or just 'Doug' which, if not 'Latham' I shall refer to him by.

These three occupants of 9 Clifton Road were to be temporarily comforted by the next-door neighbour at number 11. After a brief discussion with the police officers who first attended, it wasn't too long before they were all conveyed to Kidderminster Police Station to gain an initial appraisal of the circumstances of their home and their activities for that day.

It is here that I think we should pause in order to give the reader an additional appreciation of the scene involved and all those occupants in normal occupation of the house where the body of Mr. Davies was discovered.

2. The Scene –

As can be seen on the map shown below, the Birchen Coppice estate is not within the main conurbation of Kidderminster but almost lying mid-way between Kidderminster and Stourport-on-Severn. Both towns can be accessed from the estate well within ten minutes but Stourport is slightly further away than Kidderminster itself.

Although a smaller town than Kidderminster, Stourport is attracted by many who own and rent caravans on the banks of, or close to the River Severn, which runs through the town. The river links with a canal basin which is also frequented by barge owners as a terminal for river and canal boats and barges. There are river and canal trips to be purchased and it also has a small static funfair which attracts many from the nearby larger West Midland Conurbations.

The Birchen Coppice Estate has already been described within the introduction to this book. The specific house at 9 Clifton Road, had been described by those entering it, as dirty, and smelly and overrun by four small terrier-type dogs (one blind) and a cat. They were said to roam free to the unkempt garden in order to leave their excrement there. The garden contained many pieces of scrap metal, which the deceased bought and sold to make extra money on top of the income from his regular job as a refuse collector. (More on that later)

This semi-detached house was built and owned by the Local Authority about 20 years prior to this murder. The Davies' took advantage of the Local Authority's assisted mortgage scheme and purchased the house for £9,000 in January, 1980, about a year prior to Mr. Davies' death. A side entry gate and a brick wall divided the front garden from the rear and served to keep the dogs in the rear garden. The back door to the house was normally kept ajar in order to give the animals free rein, whether the house is occupied or not.

All visitors used the rear door to gain access to the house, for one reason: the front door had been stuck closed for a very long time and was extremely difficult to open. indeed, it could only be opened from the outside by use of extreme force. For that reason, callers unaware of that situation were directed to use the side gate to access the door at the side. On hearing the opening of this side gate, the four dogs routinely rushed out barking to greet whoever it was who opened it.

The below map is reproduced courtesy of 'Google Maps'.

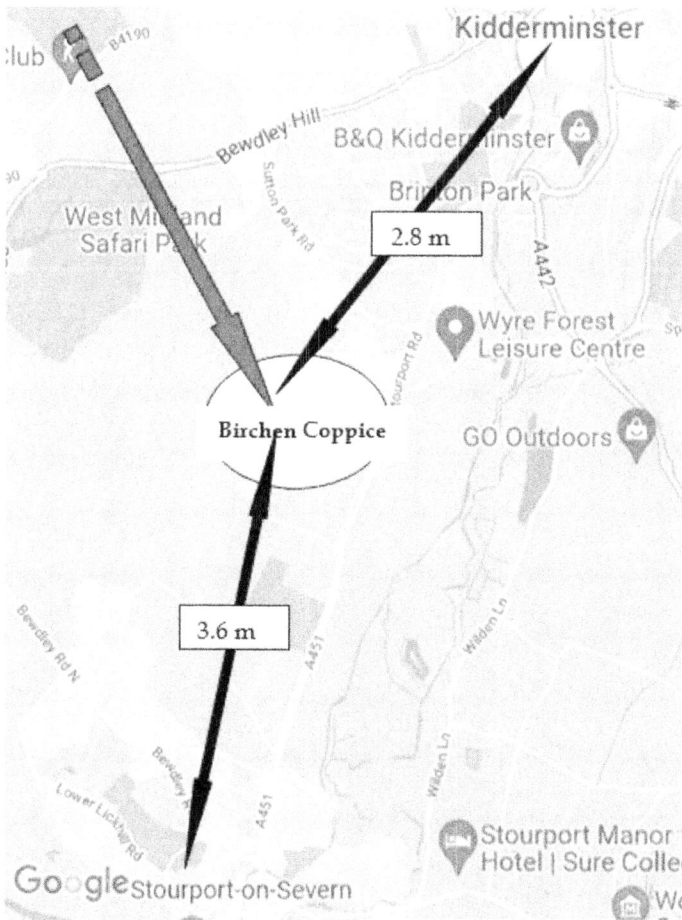

**9 Clifton Road on the left next door to number 11 on the right.
Image captured by Google Maps in 2012.**

The property comprises a kitchen, living room and hallway on the ground floor and a bathroom and three bedrooms on the first floor.

The deceased, John Davies, had been lying on a settee in front of a lit fire in the living room. From the prone position in which he had been found, it was apparent that he had been asleep at the time he was attacked. His shoes had been removed and so he was lying on his right side with his head closest to the front of the house. His head had been attacked with such ferocity that brain matter was protruding from his cranium.

3. The deceased – Arthur John Davies

For a start, we need to overcome some difficulties with regard to the names of the occupants of the house. It might have been suspected that Mr Davies's wife, Betty, may have been born an Elizabeth but her birth was in fact registered as simply, Betty; so, no change there.

For whatever reason, the remaining occupants had some quirk or other, resulting in either their names being slightly different when compared with that provided when their births were first officially registered, or, in John's case, the location where he was born and the identity of his parents. I readily concede that whilst these questions may not be pertinent to the fact of who it was that killed him, I believe that knowing the background of the participants involved, they help to set the scene.

Mr Davies was always referred to by all who knew him as John, which is his second Christian name. They would not know him by his first Christian name of Arthur. He was sometimes referred to as 'Dusty' Davies or 'Dustbin' Davies, these nicknames having a bearing on his occupation as a dustman. It will therefore be more appropriate to refer to him from now on as John, and not Arthur.

In addition, if it was not his parents that raised him at Martley, a village some twelve miles from Kidderminster, the name DAVIS, i.e., without the additional 'E' as in DAVIES, does become pertinent. However, time has either witnessed their family name acquiring that letter 'e' or could it be that another family of DAVIES or DAVIS raised him? So far as the spelling of the name is concerned, I have made the decision to stick with the name DAVIES, in relation to John and his family, which is the name always used by them.

So far as the others are concerned, if necessary, I shall deal with their names when I come to describe them.

The birth and early childhood of John in itself, has caused its own enigma. According to his wife, Betty, who, apart from their daughter, Caroline, was the only available informant with a little knowledge of John's family, he suffered quite a deprived childhood. She states that he was born in Lime Street, London, but there is no evidence to support that fact whatsoever. On the contrary, research made forty years later suggests that he was born in Worcester, where some of his six siblings were born.

It wasn't until research into this book began that the retrieval of his birth certificate from the General Register Office was to conclusively prove that he was, indeed, born in the Tallow Hill Maternity Unit at Shrub Hill Worcester - by coincidence, the same place where my youngest daughter was born.

As an aside, this building was very austere and could even in my memory, so easily be a reminder that it was once a part of the old Worcester Union Workhouse. Since then, one of the few parts of it remaining, was converted into the St Paul's hostel for the homeless. In 1986, it was finally demolished and a new hostel built on the same site.

The Birth Registration for an Arthur J. Davies was discovered as is shown below, under the surname spelt as DAVIES.

— Arthur	Overton	Birmingham	S. 6 d	175
— Arthur J.	Rowlands	Builth	11 b	76
— Arthur J.	Watts	Worcester	6 c	200
— Arthur V.	Prosser	Bridgend	11 a	1081

Betty related the fact that John apparently had six siblings, Barbara, Pamela, Pat, Edna, Albert and Paul but in what order they were born, she was unable to say. Her knowledge of his family was very scant and she said that apart from a sister, Pamela, who they visited in Bristol three years prior to his murder, neither of them had made any contact with his other siblings during the whole of their married lives.

Betty volunteered the fact that John's parents abandoned him and his siblings when he was about seven and he was looked after by his aunt and uncle, Frederick and Beatrice Grubb, at Martley. She also said that all his siblings were sent to an unknown orphanage. A similar version of

John's early life was given by Carol when she first provided her written statement, after she had been conveyed to the police station. However, she added that her father was seven when he had been adopted. (1939) She didn't know any of her father's siblings, but thought that Barbara was in Manchester and both Pat and Edna were in Worcester. She also stated that Pamela was nursing in Bristol and that all she knew of her dad's brother, Paul, was that he lived somewhere in Wales. She never mentioned Albert.

The surname DAVIS had also been searched but to no avail. As can be seen from the birth register above, the name 'WATTS' was in fact the maiden name given by John's mother at the time she registered his birth. The fact that it is 'WATTS' is confirmed on John's birth certificate below, as it was with the registrations of his siblings, Edna and Barbara.

CERTIFIED COPY OF AN ENTRY OF BIRTH

REGISTRATION DISTRICT				WORCESTER	
1932 BIRTH in the Sub-district of Worcester				in the Counties	
Columns	1	2	3	4	5	6
No.	When and where born	Name, if any	Sex	Name and surname of father	Name, surname and maiden surname of mother	Occupation of father
424	Seventeenth February 1932 1·A· Tallow Hill U·D	Arthur John	Boy	Sidney Albert Davies	Beatrice Olive Davies formerly Watts	Farm Labourer 1. Bungalow Wichenford hartley R.D.

B. O. Davies
mother
1· Bungalow
Wichenford

Sixteenth
march
1932

Showing the important entries in the birth certificate of Arthur John Davies, son of Sidney Albert and Beatrice Olive Davies (nee Watts)

All this, of course, supports conclusively that John was not, as thought by his wife, born in Lime Street, London but that he was, in fact, born in Worcester and the other names provided were his siblings.

In addition, what was known positively at the time of his murder was the fact that John's birthday was on 17th February 1932. The same date as is shown on the birth certificate. So, this birth certificate most definitely refers to Betty's husband and Carol's father.

One wonders why it was that six of the children were orphaned and yet John was cared for by an aunt and uncle. He may well have been the youngest, but that is only conjecture.

A search of the genealogical indices confirmed the existence of a Frederick Thomas and Beatrice Alice Grubb, resident in 1939 at 1 Prickley Bungalow, Martley. Beatrice's maiden name was Shaw.

However, it is Frederick's mother, Mary Ann Grubb, who provides an insight as to how the name Davies is derived from John's ancestors. Mary Ann had given birth to five illegitimate children, all of course, given the name of Grubb. Her first, Ursula was born in March 1881. The census of that year was taken when the baby was just one month old and both mother and baby having no support, were found in the Martley Union Workhouse.

Only three years later on 28th May 1884, Mary Ann appeared before Worcester Magistrates charged with attempting to conceal the birth of a dead female child which she delivered on 4th April at St. Johns, Worcester. She was tried on 24th July 1884 and found not guilty. Still a single girl, she then gave birth to four sons as follows: -

- 28th March 1886 - William Samuel Grubb

- October 1889 – Ernest Christopher Grubb

- 8th December 1891 – **Frederick Thomas Grubb** (The subsequent Guardian of John Davies)

- July 1893 – Sidney Albert Grubb

So, with five surviving children and one who died as an infant, Mary Ann had also survived the workhouse with her first born, Ursula in 1881 and, apparently, with no permanent man by her side. She must therefore have been a little relieved when along came a 'Mr. Right', a certain William DAVIS (Not DAVIES) who was now a widower, having lost his first wife, Emma Kettle. She died in 1885 at the time of the birth of their first and only child, Fanny, just five years after their marriage.

William Davis was a Martley man and he then married Mary Ann Grubb in January 1895. He of course took on all her children, including Frederick Thomas Grubb, born 1891, who later became the surrogate father of our deceased victim, Arthur John Davies.

One is bound to wonder whether he was in fact the father of her illegitimate babies. It wasn't long before Mary Ann started to give birth again. They married during the first quarter of 1895 and in the 2nd quarter, their first child, Arthur John Davies was born. (Oh NO! Yes, this is exactly the same name as our deceased, the murdered Arthur John Davies) – of course, now known as John. They went on to have two more children, Amy Rosamond (Rose,) born 1897, and Edith May, born 1900.

One would immediately lean towards this Arthur John Davies as being the father of the deceased by the same name, but, unfortunately, he was killed as a single man in World War 1 during 1917. 15 years before our John Davies was even born in 1932.

It is because this Davis family at Martley were John's aunt and uncle, then the most acceptable solution to this enigma is that it would be one of these guardians' siblings who would have been either his paternal or maternal parent. He could well have been named after his deceased's name-sake or one of his siblings.

Without an even deeper genealogical investigation which, in relation to this book, the conundrum doesn't really warrant, we shall never know. Suffice to say that Mary Ann Grubb, undoubtedly married into one of John's ancestors and whoever he was, she had given birth to nine children by two men and died at Martley in 1947. aged 86.

So finally, we can possibly find the answer to this conundrum. We know that John was born, as his birth certificate states, to a Sidney Albert Davies and a Beatrice Olive Watts in 1932.

On the other hand, it has been stated that he was adopted when he was seven and luckily, that would be in 1939 - the year that the national register was taken in preparation for identity cards to be issued, prior to the onset of World War Two. For information, only the particulars of people who have since died, are permitted to be viewed and any without such evidence are blanked out and called 'CLOSED'.

In the 1939 Register at Martley Subdivision 3761, Code QKJT is discovered at 4, Malvern View Bungalows. John's birth parents as stated above with four records of children being 'closed' but with one open, being John's sibling, Barbara, who was born on 7th May 1929.

The additional but separate Martley Subdivision 3761, Code QKJT register contains the entries for, lo and behold, Frederick Thomas Grubb and his wife Beatrice Alice Grubb (nee DAVIS) resident at 'Prickley Cottage' Martley - the family alleged to have adopted John when he was seven. Their entry does not contain any children, alive or dead so it is assumed that he and his siblings were abandoned at around that 1939 period.

So, there we have it, John was indeed, born at Worcester and raised at Martley for the whole of his childhood, but it is alleged that, when he was about seven, his mother abandoned him and his siblings and he was then raised alone by another Martley family, not far from his family home. This family's name was Grubb but his adopted father's mother's maiden name was 'DAVIS'.

So, having ascertained the circumstances of John's early sad life, we must now paint the picture of what sort of a man he was, following his marriage and prior to his murder. Getting straight to the point, he wasn't a popular man and was thought of by many as a drunkard and a bully and forceful enough to get what he wanted. However, he idolised his only child, his daughter Caroline Beatrice, who was known by all who knew her as 'Carol', so that is the name by which I shall continue to refer to her. Both he and his daughter were said to have quick tempers.

Pausing here for a second, it will not go unnoticed that John's birth mother's name was Beatrice Olive and the lady who later raised him as his guardian or surrogate mother, was his aunty Beatrice (nee Shaw). There can be little doubt therefore, that his daughter Carol Beatrice, carried their 'Beatrice' family names.

John was a chargehand refuse collector and nicknamed 'Dusty' or 'Dustbin Davies'. He was said to possess a strong forceful personality, being inclined to be aggressive and boastful. He wasn't liked by his colleagues who believed, rightly or wrongly, that he was favoured by the bosses at the Council yard as the one who got all the overtime and was permitted to take the scrap metal from the bins on a weekend and who, to add insult to their injury, was getting paid overtime for doing so. It was also suggested that he would either give or sell bottles of whisky at discount prices to his bosses to allow these practices to happen and to curry favour with them at times when disciplinary action loomed over him.

Such complaints concerned his dustcart being observed to be outside a public house during a lunchtime drinking spree.

Another complaint of drunkenness involved allegations by his colleagues that he was dealt with by means of a verbal warning at work, instead of being properly disciplined. Complaints had been made by members of the public concerning him falling over in a drunken state on his bin round. On 7th January 1981, 20 days prior to his death, he was interviewed at work by his supervisors. His fall was attributed to the icy conditions which prevailed at the time.

He had been a shop steward and on one occasion was suspended from driving for six months by a senior council officer who later alleged that Davies had been too leniently dealt with on the previous occasion.

It must be made clear here that, although it is of little significance to this murder investigation, a separate and independent police investigation was launched into these allegations of corruption by council officials, with a view to prosecuting them for these alleged corrupt activities. The matter did go to trial at Hereford Crown Court some two years after John's death, but all cases were found not to be proved and were dismissed. However, the fact that these allegations were made helps paint the portrait of how others viewed 'Dusty Davies'.

The income Davies derived from buying and selling scrap metal was quite significant. Not only would he sell the scrap he collected during his own employment, but he would buy it from his work colleagues and from people calling at his door. From the 1980 records held at just one scrap metal merchant, he was paid almost £,5000 which was well over 50% of the income derived from his employment with the council. It was said that he was earning far more than his boss and over £2,000 more than all other Kidderminster dustmen.

Mrs Davies was able to inform us that before their marriage, John served for seven years in the parachute regiment from 1949 until 1956, his last posting being to Düsseldorf, Germany. He returned to Martley, where he was employed as a farm labourer before they married in 1957. It was her father who got John the job at the council as a dustman and he had continuously been employed as such until his death.

John had a healthy bank account and savings and frequently carried large amounts of money in his wallet, never less than £100. He was known to frequently lend money to a neighbour and his workmates.

This was 40 years ago prior to this book being written and he was known to spend freely on entertainment and alcohol. It was only the day before his death that he said that he had spent £70 on lunchtime drinks. He was the type that would 'flash' this money around to portray a man of some affluence. Home truths of him being a dustman must have hurt.

So far as his relationships with his wife and daughter were concerned, his wife Betty's description of his activities can be summarised as being supportive of him and, although he and Carol were both quick tempered and argued with each other, he would never use violence.

He always rose early and was scarcely absent from his work. Apart from his drinking habit, he worked hard to reap the benefits derived.

Despite Carol stating that it was her dad who invited Latham to move into their home, it appeared that John never savoured the prospect of Latham moving in with his family at all. Latham wouldn't have been aware as to how he was going to have to contend with John's possessive jealousy and also his scheming, devious character of extreme cunning who, with a reputation as a small-time police informer, almost succeeded in outwitting Latham at his own game and only failed at the hand of extreme violence. More on that aspect later.

4. Betty Davies (nee Larking)

John's wife, Betty and an elder brother, Ronald, were the only children of Sidney George Larking and Florence Elizabeth (nee Hartwell). They were born at Kidderminster.

Birth registrations suggest that their father was an illegitimate boy born in the Marylebone workhouse, London, as Sydney George Larkin. (A difference in spelling of both Christian and surnames)

It is believed that he moved to Kidderminster prior to 1936 where he was employed at the RAF station, Hartlebury as a General Labourer. He met Betty's mother, 'Florrie' Hartwell and they married in the July of 1936, almost two years before Betty was born at the time when they lived at 19 Goldthorn Road, a matter of about a 15-minute walk from Betty's home at Clifton Road.

On Betty's maternal side, both her father and her grandfather were Kidderminster people whose families were mostly employed in the carpet manufacturing process. Her father was a 'Wool Weaver' and Betty herself was a 'Carpet Winder', an occupation in which she was employed when her husband was murdered. She was then 42 years of age and her place of employment was situated about a mile from her home in Clifton Road.

Betty's working hours were from 8am until 3.30pm on a full-time basis but with her husband leaving for work before her, in recent times, the only people left in the house would be her daughter and her boyfriend, Douglas Latham who moved into their home in about October 1980. He was unemployed but was casually employed as a barman at The Bridge Inn, Mill Street, Kidderminster.

Betty discovered her husband's body at 3.50pm on 27th January 1981 on arriving home from work.

5. – Other Occupants of 9 Clifton Road – Caroline Beatrice Davies

Caroline, now to be referred to as Carol, was born at a Kidderminster maternity home on 29th March 1960, she was 21 at the time of her father's death. She had lived at Clifton Road with her parents since she was 11 years of age.

Carol first went to Summerfield Church of England School Hartlebury before attending St John's Junior School, Kidderminster. Her final school was the Secondary Modern School, The Harry Cheshire School, now known as Baxter College.

On leaving school, she worked at a local pet shop but left in May 1978. She remained unemployed for a year when she went to work as a cashier at the West Midlands Safari Park. It was there, not long after her employment commenced, that she met Douglas Latham. It wasn't long after their relationship started that, in November 1980, they both became unemployed and when Latham moved in to live with her family. They both remained unemployed up until the time of her father's death on 27th January, 1981.

She was a girl who would appear to have led an uneventful life until she met her boyfriend, Latham. It wasn't long after he had moved into the Davies family home that friction between the deceased, John Davies and the couple developed. She proved to be just as scheming an individual as her father and was surprisingly quickly taken in by Latham's persuasiveness and the expectations of financial rewards from enterprises they were supposedly to embark upon.

She has been described as an unattractive girl, but, although she possessed a limited education, she had a strength of character and cunning, with an unshakeable loyalty towards Latham in favour of him as opposed to her own parents.

6. - Douglas Iorworth William Ellis Casey LATHAM

The facts of Latham's origins are clouded, inasmuch as at the time of his birth, details of his immediate family were largely unknown. Doubtless, he had a poor background and what can be ascertained is that, after his birth and early years in London, he was raised for a long period by his grandmother who resided at 11, Gilgal, Stourport-on-Severn. Unfortunately, his grandparents were deceased at the time of the murder thus depriving an independent insight into their grandson's early life.

Much of what is known since his birth on 10th August 1953 is as a result of word of mouth or 'hearsay', lacking any official documentation. However, as shown on the last line below, the section of the birth register for the third quarter of 1953 is a factual document, though it still cannot guarantee accuracy.

CASEMORE, Christine	LEACH	Coventry	9	c	990
CASEY, Angela	BENSON	Claro	2	c	91
— Ann	MAREE	Merthyr T.	8	b	538
— Ann A.	PARKIN	Durham N.W.	1	a	696
— Annette	ROBERTS	Wrexham	8	a	441
— Bernard N.	JONES	Middlesex S.	5	f	86
— Brian	HART	Liverpool S.	10	d	825
— Calwin A.	WILLIAMS	Bangor	8	a	67
— Calvin B.	STOCKWELL	Lambeth	5	c	1662
— Cecilia	CASEY	Leeds	2	c	201
— Charles	BRUFORD	Cardiff	8	b	154
— Christine	DAVIDSON	Durham S.E.	1	a	799
— David	McINTYRE	Ormskirk	10	f	231
— David A.	CASEY	Ealing	5	e	145
— Denise M.	JUDGE	Crosby	10	c	106
— Derek W.A.	BATEMAN	Wigan	10	f	972
— Douglas I.W.E.	CLANFORD	Paddington	5	d	275

For a start, it tells us that his name wasn't Latham after all, (see first line of the register above) but that it was CASEY, a name which was subsequently transformed to form his fifth Christian name. The surname LATHAM must have been added some time after the registration.

What could have been of interest, was that the entry indicates that his mother's maiden name was 'CLANFORD' and the registration was made in the district of Paddington.

Normally, with genealogy being the author's hobby, one might expect there to be other births under her maiden name CLANFORD or indeed, that of LATHAM OR CASEY.

The name 'CLANFORD' is comparatively unusual, but, unfortunately, detailed searches made for a period stretching for five years either side of the 1953 registration have failed to unearth any similar births relating to either of the CLANFORD, CASEY or LATHAM surnames.

Latham's factual life as known since then, includes the marriage to two local girls. His first marriage was at 18 years of age in early 1974. His daughter was born just less than two years prior to the marriage. A son was born a few months following the marriage.

He often left the marital home apparently, to look for work. In that vein, he went to Scotland and then towards the end of their marriage, he left his wife and two children to work in Germany. Whilst he kept in touch by letter, his wife finally asked him for a divorce and it was then that he disclosed a further relationship. They were divorced two years later, but he has since never financially contributed towards the maintenance of their home, his wife or the two children he fathered in this relationship.

He then remarried in January 1979 but separated from his second wife later that same year. By the time John's murder had been committed, divorce proceedings had already been instigated. Both wives were in agreement about most aspects of his character in that he was a 'romancer', who always nurtured dreams of making a lot of money.

For one reason or another, he rarely kept any job long and was simply not prepared to undertake regular, steady employment. He developed some skill as a welder / plater and regularly travelled to Germany, ostensibly to undertake contracts but often he returned with work not having materialised.

By nature, Latham is a boastful man who seems attracted by life in the armed services and has often bragged about being a mercenary in Angola. He also allegedly served in the Special Air Service (SAS) as a paratrooper.

In reality he served in the local Territorial Army for 26 months.

Another feature of his character which attracts comment is his tendency to hypochondria. He appears to have been a frequent visitor to the local hospital outpatient's department without good reason.

It soon became known that Latham had become a lifelong failure who coveted elaborate and grandiose plans for his own future, all of which failed to materialise. This was mainly because he was too idle to put the necessary effort into his ambitions. He could quite accurately be described as a 'Walter Mitty' character. It soon became clear that he was an inveterate liar and had used this dubious talent in the past to exaggerate his own importance and to cheat and steal for his own ends.

So far as his honesty is concerned, as a Juvenile aged 14, he had already appeared before the justices at Stourport and been placed on probation for two years for 'Theft' on the first occasion and then 'Store Breaking' (2 cases) and stealing wine and beer on the other.

On 7th August 1972, he was convicted of driving a motor vehicle without insurance and was fined and disqualified from driving for 6 months.

On 8th January 1974, he failed to report that he had been involved in a road accident and was again fined and disqualified from driving for another 6 months.

On 24th September 1974 he was convicted of assisting in the retention of stolen goods and the fraudulent use of a 'Road Excise Licence', failing to display 'L' plates and driving without insurance again. He was fined a total of £60 for all these offences and once again, disqualified from driving for 12 months.

On 23rd September 1980, approximately four months before the murder of John Davies, he was convicted of burglary and theft with two other offences taken into consideration. He was sentenced to three months imprisonment, suspended for a year and ordered to pay compensation.

In summary, Latham was a rather unsavoury character with no respect for the law or anyone else except himself.

He appeared to be a man with a chip on his shoulder, a man with big ideas and ambitions but who, in the end, achieved nothing.

7. - Early Sequential events

With the benefit of hindsight and the above information now being presented, readers might be forgiven for believing that Latham and his girlfriend Carol, should immediately be detained as suspects involved in this brutal killing or at least, would have somehow been implicated with the murder.

I would also be lying if my thoughts hadn't also drifted to that early conclusion. However, it would, of course, be wrong to jump to any conclusion at all. In any event, there are advantages in treating people who, although they might fall under suspicion at a later stage, in the early stages of any criminal investigation, should be treated as evidential witnesses.

This is the opportunity for them to tell the investigators exactly what they want to tell them. If they were involved, but not suspected to be, then they would hardly refuse to answer questions. On the contrary, they would want to tell the investigators as much as they could, which would allay any suspicions from falling their way.

And so, there was a period when that which was required to be performed at the scene, had been done. The scene and body in situ had been dealt with both medically and forensically. The 'scenes of crime' investigators had completed their thorough examination of the scene and the Home Office pathologist, Dr. Norman Gower was asked to perform the post-mortem operation on John's body at Kidderminster hospital.

All that remained was for us senior investigating officers and the supporting team to put into place, as quickly as possible, all the cogs in the wheel which are required to be set, so that the wheel is put into motion to establish whoever it was had killed John Davies.

The living room where John was killed was, to put it politely, required to be 'attended' to. Also, the four dogs and the cat they owned, were required to be looked after until Mrs Davies was free to organise such steps. In short, there came a time when the natural course of events would soon lead to the Investigating Officers wanting to arrange house-to-house enquiries to gather information and ascertain if any of the neighbours had seen any activity at all at the house.

In that vein, such enquiries were put into train almost immediately and various statements were recorded concerning activities in or near the scene.

Early interviews at the scene

The obvious priority was the necessity to speak to the three other occupants of the house – Betty was of course the first person to know of her husband's death when she found him in that awful condition already described. Her daughter, Carol, and her boyfriend, Douglas Latham, had arrived on the scene in Carol's silver Vauxhall Viva car at 4.25pm when the police were already in attendance.

As other occupants of the house, it was, of course, vital to gain an early appreciation of their whereabouts on that day and the sequence of their events. Carol appeared to be crying hysterically and Latham asked Sergeant Jones what had happened.

Fortunately, with the murder having taken place in the house where they resided, these three people understood that they would be required to assist the investigating officers and so they were later conveyed to the police station variously at times not too long after the grim discovery.

However, the first police officer to discuss the movements of those from number 9, who were then being consoled next door in number 11 Clifton Road, was Sergeant Wyndham Jones. Discussions with them were made in the presence and hearing of the others, though most questions were directed at Latham who was the more composed of the three.

Sgt. Jones was doing the right thing in an effort to find out what this was all about. Had he known that Latham and Carol might be involved, then he wouldn't have questioned them as a group, as one suspect would of course, get to know what the other was saying and would simply 'follow their suit' with their own answers.

Latham indicated that John would have left for work first, before Mrs Davies, (Betty) left for her work and that both he and Carol were the last to leave the house at between 11am and 11.30am, in order to take Carol to the dentists in Lion Street.

However, he said that, prior to them leaving the house, John returned home and they left after a brief chat with him.

Caroline (Carol) confirmed that version and that after leaving the dentists, they both went to the Bridge Inn, Mill Street, where Latham occasionally helped out behind the bar.

It is as well to indicate here, that this pub, 'The Bridge Inn' was to be the establishment which will feature quite often, where boasts were to be made, seeds of conspiracy were to be sown and the grandiose schemes including Latham's plans to emigrate to South Africa with Carol, were to be discussed.

Sergeant Jones continued to ask questions of these three occupants of number 9. One can perhaps imagine how awkward that would be with both Betty and her daughter Carol, crying on the settee, and Latham kneeling besides them. He ascertained that Latham was engaged to Carol and that he was living in the house next door, with this Davies family.

Sergeant Jones then asked Latham when it was that he last saw Mr Davies. He was told that they both returned home at about 2pm. He described John as lying on the settee trying to have a sleep. He then said, "We all had a chat and he gave us £2 for petrol and we then left." He indicated that they left at about 2.15pm when John had been alive and well.

Latham also volunteered to Sgt. Jones that John had been 'on the sick' after falling at work on some ice and also that he had been involved in a dispute with some of his workmates at work and with a security officer there. When asked if he knew of any reason why anyone would want to kill John. He could not, except he said, that they had been receiving telephone calls whereby the line went dead after being answered.

On another occasion a man was asking for 'Arthur' Davies and not by the name John which everyone knew him by. The call was about a 'building' which didn't make sense.

So, as far as Sergeant Jones was concerned, Latham stated that he last saw John at 2.15pm when they left the house having 'cadged' £2 off him for petrol. At no time did he mention that they returned to the house for any other reason.

After agreeing to be taken to the police station, Latham was conveyed there by Detective Sergeant Griffiths and Detective Constable McIntosh, arriving at about 5.20pm. Caroline was later taken to the police station at 7pm by Detective Inspector Herbert and Policewoman Detective Constable Gwyther.

Early Interviews at Kidderminster Police Station – The procedures.

With so many police procedural scenes being shown on television these days, I suspect that most who view them will know as much as I do about the relative procedures. For the purposes of this book however, I had better explain that being interviewed at the police station by a police officer would normally involve one of two types of interviews and in some cases, such as this case in question, the people being interviewed could be questioned under both procedures.

The 'not so serious' types of interviews are referred to as witness interviews and any statement recorded in connection with the questions being asked, would, in most cases, be written as 'witness statements' by the officer conducting the interview.

Contrary to what people might believe from the media, these witness statements can, and most always are, structured by the officer asking questions of the witness. This ensures that all the background and necessary elements of what needs to be proved, can be included in the statement so long as the maker of it can testify that what the statement includes is his or her account of what actually happened. Such examples might include people who have seen a fight or a road accident.

There have been allegations made about the police changing statements to suit their case. Whilst this may have been the case in some notorious instances, there have been many allegations about the changing of statements which have involved this type of procedure. It's so often happened when things go 'pear-shaped' for the person making the statement or when they wish to gain some advantage from such an allegation.

They may well have gilded the lily or even told untruths but when fingers are pointed, they then recall how the statement was structured and blame the police for writing it.

They will have conveniently forgotten that after the statement was concluded, they read it through and signed it by stating in a form of a certification, that they had made it of their own free will and that so far as they are aware, it is the truth and that they had been asked if they wished to correct, alter or add anything they wished.

Interview Skills

The skills of interviewing were never taught in my day and most likely are not taught today. It is a procedure which, apart from fundamentals, would be difficult to teach in a classroom. I wouldn't have been the best interviewer in the world but consider that I was privileged to have been present in many interviews being conducted by seasoned officers when I first gained experience in the CID, as a young constable undertaking an attachment as an 'aide to CID'.

In particular, Detective Sergeant Phil Paton was a master. It was he who 'tucked me under his arm' in many interviews. There was never any banging on the desk or shouting at the suspect. He may not even have sat and planned the interview beforehand, though I suspect that he had thought them through. He was so quick witted and simply outthought and outsmarted his adversaries.

Some officers have particular penchants for different aspects of policing. In the 'Detective' world, my boss of the day, David Cole, was particularly keen on forensic evidence, including that derived from post-mortem examinations. This was before DNA science and mobile phone technology hit the headlines and I know if he had been alive and working in these days, he would have been all over these sciences and technologies like a rash.

It was thanks to Phil Paton that one of my particular interests was simply 'interviewing'. I recall in the report Phil wrote about my attachment, that I was inclined to 'give away' too much information to those being interviewed. I knew exactly what he meant and have never forgotten it. That is a simple example and I think one can only learn to improve interview technique with practice and planning.

I grew to be proud that on occasions, particularly when I had reached the DCI (Detective Chief Inspector) rank at Malvern and at Worcester, I would be asked, or very occasionally received a phone call at home from a station asking me if I would "have a go" at particular suspects who were 99% known to be responsible for what they had been arrested for, but just would not 'cough up'. I wasn't always successful but boy, what a buzz is experienced when they do 'cough'. I think I found my penchant.

In this case, neither Latham or Carol would have been classed as suspects during their initial interviews and therefore they were witnesses. This means that they were at the police station voluntarily and would not get searched, placed in handcuffs, charged or locked up. Can I hear tones amounting to –Ohhhhh Yes!

I will therefore add that those conducting the interviews might well form a gut reaction or even a rough idea that the interviewee is hiding something or acting in a suspicious or nervous way. So, feeling that someone might be guilty without any evidence which indicates that guilt, would not be strong enough 'per se' to treat the witness as a suspect. It could be different if they provide accounts which, according to evidence already at hand, were so untrue. So, what is the difference?

The major difference is that when evidence exists which causes a police officer to suspect that the person to be, or is being interviewed, is responsible for a criminal offence, then that person should be cautioned by use of the following words: -

"You are not obliged to say anything unless you wish to do so but what you say may be put into writing and given in evidence".

This procedure was laid down in what was known as, 'The Judges' Rules' which were not law but designed as guidance to treat suspects fairly in that their right of silence should be respected.

Hearing the caution would obviously put the recipient 'on guard' and he or she might well, at that stage, wish to have a solicitor present, or simply say, "No COMMENT". (Or both)

If the interviewee was suspected before being arrested then they would receive that caution as soon as they were arrested and also at the time when they were charged with the offence.

If witnesses being interviewed as witnesses subsequently cause the interviewer to suspect that he or she is a suspect, then as soon as that suspicion is formed, then the officer should caution the suspect in the above terms. The administration of the caution would not automatically mean that the suspect would be under arrest or would be searched. Those decisions would be made dependent on how the interview progressed and the nature of the crime and the evidence gathered etc.

I might add that the Police and Criminal Act of 1984 caused the caution to be slightly amended but here, we are dealing with procedures, three years prior to this legislation being introduced.

Witness Interview – Douglas Latham

In answering questions put to him by Detective Sergeant Griffiths, Latham informed him that he and Carol rose at about 10am and were then alone in the house because John and Betty had already left for work.

He repeated that they visited the dentists in Lion Street, where Carol had had some teeth extracted, but before they had left home for the dentist, John arrived home at about 11.15am and that following a short chat, they then left for the dentists at about 11.30am. He said that they had arrived early at the dentists and that not having been there for too long, they departed to the Bridge Inn at Mill Street, arriving there at just after 12 noon.

They would have spent just under a couple of hours in the pub before getting home at about 2.15pm, where Carol 'cadged' £2 off her dad for petrol.

Despite being given the impression that the back door is always left open, for some reason, Latham told DS Griffiths that he gave John their back door key because he said that he, (John) was going to go out.

One wonders therefore why John didn't have a key of his own or in any event, why he wanted to lock the door on his going out, when it was said to be routinely left open.

When asked what he was going to do next, Latham introduced another of their companions to the equation, a certain Danny McLaughlin who will, of course, be used a little later to corroborate or deny Latham's whereabouts on that day.

Danny lived with his girlfriend and their three-year-old baby daughter at 56 Grasmere Close. Their objective of making this visit was that the men could discuss a darts match to be played on the following day.

They drank a coffee and left after about half an hour. But, before we extend the lines of inquiry to Danny McLaughlin and other people, let us first complete the description of their day by looking at Carol's version of events during this same period. Again, I stress that this was just a matter of hours after the death of Carol's father and so their movements should have been fresh in their minds.

1st Interview of Caroline (Carol) Davies. (As detailed by her)

This would be the first of many 'official' interviews held with Carol since Sergeant Jones attempted to gauge what had happened to the 9 Clifton Road occupants that day, when he spoke to Carol at their neighbour's house, at number 11.

She was brought to the police station later that evening so that her movements for the day and background information of members of the household could be recorded. It was following the giving of her account to Detective Inspector Herbert and DPW Gwyther that she recorded a witness statement written by DPW Gwyther in the presence of Det. Insp. Herbert. This procedure lasted a total of six hours and twenty-five minutes and terminated at 2.05am the next day. With no tape recording or videoing of interviews in those days, it was important to have her account recorded in such a statement.

In summary, Carol provided much of the background to the domestic situation which prevailed in her home at that time. She described how she and Latham first got together and him moving in to live with her family. At first, he was unemployed but was then employed on shift work as a 'slicer' at the local sugar beet factory, when he was then lodging with a friend, Alan Hardiman at 124 Walter Nash Road, Kidderminster.

Walter Nash Road is an arterial road running through the Birchen Coppice Estate and Clifton Road is a turning leading from it.

She said that it was owing to the difficulties with his shifts upsetting the situation at this household, that her father asked him to live at their family home. They both paid Carol's mother £14 per week for their keep.

However, Latham was soon unemployed after going sick for a couple of weeks and then they went to Wales for a few days before returning to find a letter which informed Doug that he had been sacked for absenteeism. Carol then described a typical day for her and Doug which started at between 10am and 11am when they rose from their beds.

Much of their time was spent planning to emigrate to South Africa in August of that year, where he could gain employment. Following the completion of some housework, she said that they would leave the house to go to The Bridge Inn, Mill Street at between 11am to midday and stay there until about 3pm to return back home.

At about 7.30pm, they would return to the Bridge Inn until closing time or beyond. The lateness of their return home time would be between 11pm and 2am which depended on whether or not they had a meal.

With a view to gauging who it was that might have killed her father, Carol then went on to describe the many and various people who called at their house to sell scrap metal to her dad. In addition to his work colleagues and neighbours, some were of the gypsy type. He had been involved in the scrap metal business ever since she could remember. She commented that most would call in the afternoons after her dad had returned home from work at about midday.

On the day in question, there was nothing dissimilar to a typical day described above, except that, on this occasion, they needed to visit the dentists for Carol to attend a midday appointment. They sat around the house and Doug was fiddling with his watch as he was having trouble with it. Carol described that at between 11am and 11.30am her father returned from work in his white Rover car. They were just about to leave for Carol's dental appointment, so after passing some pleasantries, Doug drove them to attend the dentists.

Doug parked the car behind Woolworth's store in the town and they attended a Mr. Mike's dental surgery in Lion Street, a short walk away, arriving there at about 11.45am. Following her having eight teeth extracted, they left the surgery at about 12.20pm to 12.30pm. Having returned to Carol's car, she remained in it whilst Doug walked through Woolworths to attend David Edwards' Jewellery shop where apparently, his watch was fixed. She says that he returned within five minutes.

Carol then described how they took to the ring road to arrive at The Bridge Inn at about 12.45pm. There, she remembered seeing several people she knew and she named ten people. Whilst she recalled all of their Christian names, she was unable to recall all of their surnames though she was able to give indications as to who they were.

One of these, Phil Breakwell, will play a significant part in this story, but more about him later, also at the appropriate times.

Carol stated that they remained at The Bridge Inn until about 2pm, when Doug again drove them home and parked the car on the drive. They had a short conversation with her dad about her teeth extractions and Doug remained in the living room talking to him, whilst she soaked some socks in water in the kitchen.

So, when the minutiae of their day so far are considered, it was basically the same as what she described as a normal day, but containing some small differences. Despite Carol needing to go to the dentist and Doug visiting the jewellers, they still managed to reach the Bridge Inn, yet they arrived home at 2pm, a whole hour earlier than the 3pm which Carol explained as their normal average day.

From what Carol then stated, it would appear that the reason why they returned home earlier, was for them to borrow money from her dad because they needed to drive Doug to the hospital. John made some joke about funding her and owing him a thousand pounds before Christmas. He then gave Carol two pounds in notes.

It was then that John declared his intentions of taking a nap before going out and Carol therefore asked if he wanted her key, should he leave the house and return before they did. She said that this involved Doug dissuading him from leaving the key under the doormat as anyone could find it there. Doug continued that he would knock the bolt off the front door. Indeed, she said that Doug withdrew the bolt on the inside of the door, whilst Carol took the key off her keyring.

The significance here is not only the fact that it had been earlier reported that it was common practice to leave the side door open for the dogs to do their business, but also with the front door being inoperative due to it being stuck in place and difficult to open other than by using some force from the outside.

It therefore wasn't unusual for the house to be left insecure with at least one means of entering it by anyone calling and, of course, anyone left inside the house would then be left vulnerable. In other words, it was questionable as to why the situation warranted the leaving of Carol's key as described.

They then left Carol's dad lying on the settee on his right side, facing the coal fire with his head closest to the front window in exactly the same position as he was later discovered. She said that it was on her dad's instructions that she left the key on the mantel shelf.

After explaining that neither Doug or herself had cause to go upstairs, she described how they left the house by the side door and how she left it slightly ajar for the dogs to leave and re-enter the house.

Although not said, the inference here is that this was in order whilst her father was in the house. As mentioned above, in a variation to their average day, they left the house at about 2pm to drive to Danny McLaughlin's house. However, before reaching his house, they stopped at the 'Minster' Self Service Petrol Station, where Doug filled the car with £2 worth of petrol and Carol went to the office to pay the £2.

Carol said that it was just after putting the petrol in the car that Doug suggested going to see their friend, Danny McLaughlin, to see if he was going to play in the darts team at the Bridge Inn on the following day. This was due to Doug being the team's vice captain, but again, this was in deference to the priority for the need for him to go to the hospital.

They arrived at Danny's home, 56 Grasmere, Horsefair at about 2.30pm to 2.35pm. She explained that he lived with his girlfriend, Lorraine, who was there with her sister Carol and Danny's child aged 2 years. They drank coffee and Doug spoke to McLaughlin about the darts match and they left after about 15 to 20 minutes.

The interview of Latham and the recording of Carol's statement went on for much longer periods but as mentioned earlier concerning Latham's early interview, we can pause here because we have reached almost exactly the same point in this interview with Carol as was earlier reached when Latham was being interviewed by Detective Sergeant Griffiths.

The purpose of this hiatus is twofold –

1. To examine how each of them explained in their own words, their relationships and movements on the day and-

2. To introduce two other parties involved in this story now mentioned, Danny Latham and Phil Breakwell.

As might be expected, with the order of events only being a few hours prior to their interviews, their movements shouldn't have been difficult for them to explain. By the same token, if they had been involved in John's murder and needed an alibi, it wouldn't be a surprise that each version matched the others.

So, in order to emphasise that the first interviews of both Latham and Carol which were conducted separately at the Police Station were to go on for longer than indicated above, it will have been noticed that there was not any material disparity between their accounts, other than that it departed from the normal day as Carol described in that on their way to the pub, she had eight teeth extracted and her boyfriend called at a jeweller shop to fix his watch. But despite these extra diversions, they still managed to reach the pub though they left an hour earlier at 2pm and not at 3pm which she had earlier described as their normal day.

To re-cap and in summary, after Carol's parents had set off for work, they rose late, at around 10am and prepared to attend the dentist's surgery in Kidderminster. This was part of a series of mass teeth extraction in preparation for their emigration to South Africa.

Doug was fiddling with his watch as recently he had been having trouble with it. As they were about to leave the house, John arrived from work. His plan was to take a short nap prior to going out. Carol left her key on the mantel shelf so that if they returned before her father's return, they would be able to enter the house by putting pressure on the front door, the bolt of which was released by Latham from the inside.

The benefit of letting material witnesses provide their own uninterrupted accounts is that any future deviation can be quickly identified.

So having fixed that itinerary as described by Latham and Carol in our heads, before continuing with the descriptions of their day, the time is right to simply describe the further two players who were drawn into the net of conspiracy, deception and death.

8. Other Material Persons Involved

Daniel James McLaughlin

McLaughlin is a native of Kidderminster and was born on 30th September, 1955. He was therefore two years younger than Latham and at the time of the murder, was aged 26. He was known to all as 'Danny'.

Being educated at a local comprehensive school, he left at age 15 to join the First Battalion of the Worcestershire and Sherwood Foresters Regiment as an infantryman. He purchased his discharge in 1978.

He was then employed as a driver for short periods of time but at the time of this investigation he was unemployed. Having married in 1976, he separated from his wife and at the time of the investigation, divorce proceedings were ongoing. Although he gave his parents' address, he was in fact living with his future wife, Lorraine Albutt, and their two-year-old daughter at 56 Grasmere, Horsefair, Kidderminster. They married seven years after the murder.

As a younger man, McLaughlin was convicted for dishonesty on three separate occasions between 1976-and 1979. He was fined for the offence of 'Theft from a Motor Vehicle' and later for an offence of 'Burglary'. In March of 1979 he was placed on probation after being sentenced for committing a further case of burglary. Seven months later he successfully applied for the probation order to be lifted.

Philip Robert Breakwell

Breakwell was a native of Evesham, born on 16th April 1961 and so was 20 years of age at the time of the murder. He too, was educated at a local Comprehensive School, leaving at age 15 when he joined the Army with 8 Regiment of The Royal Corps of Transport (RTC).

He resided at Kidderminster with his parents and a younger brother. He had been on home leave since 13th January and, apart from attending Carol's school, he had not met her, Latham or McLaughlin previously.

Having arrived in Kidderminster from his base in Germany, Breakwell stated that his reason for frequenting the Bridge Inn was because he found it difficult to make friends on leave periods. Indeed, it was on his way home from the Railway Station on 13th January, that he by chance, called in at the Bridge Inn.

The purpose of McLaughlin and Breakwell's inclusion here is because we have now reached the stage when these two became unwittingly involved in a conspiracy to murder. Both Latham and Carol's early accounts were suspended above at the time when they referred to their trip to call on Danny Mclaughlin.

So far as Breakwell was concerned, he had only been in the company of Latham, Carol Davies and Daniel McLaughlin for exactly two weeks prior to the murder as he had been in the Army in Münster, Germany, for a tour of duty prior to the 13th January, when he came home on leave.

Although he too had been a competitor in the 'Bragging Olympics' hosted at the Bridge Inn, he had no intentions whatsoever of being involved in the killing of John Davies. He in fact, feigned an injury so that he couldn't be involved in driving the getaway car, as was planned. When questioned after his arrest, he was entirely open about the conversations he had and was therefore bailed under the terms of Section 38(2) of The Magistrates Court Act to report back at Kidderminster Police Station at a later date.

9. First Interviews with Latham and Davies continued /-

Douglas Latham

So, Latham had reached the point where they left 9 Clifton Road having borrowed £2 for petrol from John and they drove to their friend Danny McLaughlin's home and stayed for about half an hour drinking coffee and discussing the darts match, which was to be played during the following day at Fernhill Heath, Worcester.

He then told Detective Sergeant Griffiths that he had seen a nurse at the casualty department during the previous day, because he had been suffering from pains in the chest. The pains were then recurring so they once again visited the hospital. He then explained that they went to see Phil Breakwell, the soldier on leave, but that he was out.

They then travelled to see another friend, Sheila Parry, at her home, 164 Walter Nash Road for coffee. They remained there for about another half hour before they then returned to their home at 9 Clifton Road, where they discovered the police and ambulance in attendance.

So, these were the movements which Latham described. It was then that Det. Sgt Griffiths asked Latham to go over again, exactly his movements during that day. This Latham did and they were exactly the same as his first account.

It might sound bizarre but to be sure, Sgt, Griffiths said, "Okay, once more if you don't mind". Once again, Latham went through every step of his journey that morning which was identical to that twice repeated before. However, it was then that he informed the Sergeant that he had omitted an additional occurrence. For the first time, he said that they returned to the house very shortly after they had left at around 2pm because he had forgotten something but that he could not remember what it was.

It was then that Sgt Griffiths administered the caution to Latham to the effect that he wasn't obliged to say anything. One can imagine that maybe earlier faint feelings that Latham was in some way involved were now being firmed up in the Sergeant's mind. He had already repeated his movements on three occasions and at possibly the very time, when John Davies was killed, he had somehow forgotten to say that he returned to the home to collect something.

It is now when it is useful if readers place themselves in the position of Latham, as a suspect. Why would he now, after several attempts, include the additional visit to their home? Of course, if he was involved in John's death, he may well have been seen to return. In that case, could he have thought it wise to include the visit as opposed to it being discovered by the police, which would then place himself in much deeper trouble.

However, Sgt Griffiths naturally pressed Latham as to the reason why he returned and Latham suggests that it could have been "his fags" that he had left behind. He further stated that Carol stayed in the car and that his visit was no longer than 30 seconds, just long enough to retrieve his cigarettes and that John was asleep on the settee. He explained that they had only left a couple of minutes before this return but that it didn't take John that long to "nod off".

Sgt Griffiths then ascertained from Latham that he was still wearing the same clothes as he had been wearing all day and he informed him that he would be requiring those clothes for forensic examination, because, he could well have been the last person to see John alive. Arrangements were then made for a scene of crime officer to take possession of Latham's clothes and to exchange them.

The interview continued and Latham was asked about John's relationships and upsets with his colleagues at work. In short, he described John as being unpopular, but that he could not think of any reason why anyone would want to kill him. In addition to going through Latham's movements again, many domestic issues were discussed in this interview, which provided a clearer picture of life at 9 Clifton Road. He mentioned that John did not want him to sleep with Carol and so, in spite of them using separate bedrooms, they managed to do that when he was not there or when John was asleep.

He was then asked about his own relationship with John and he said that it was a bit heated sometimes.

He said, "John couldn't understand why I wanted to go abroad to Cape Town in South Africa. I was going to get a job in engineering through an agency. The state of industry in this country is terrible. There's no trouble in getting a job abroad, I was going to get an old van and do it up and drive all down Africa."

DS Griffiths commented that he had noticed that Latham's feet were dirty, yet his hands were very clean. It was then that Latham said, "You believe I done it. Why else am I still here?"

It was during a spate of conversation that DC McIntosh also commented to Latham that having received the petrol money from John, he hadn't mentioned the obtaining of any petrol. It must be remembered that Latham had by now, gone over and over their movements that day, yet he had not mentioned the petrol. In response to this he said, "I can't remember everything, I think we called at Minster. I served myself, it's self-service."

So, although this was an occurrence of only a few hours earlier, he only 'THOUGHT' that they had called at the Minster service station. That in itself is bizarre but when he also stated that he was unable to remember who paid for the petrol or who served him, the visit becomes very doubtful especially having regard to the fact that this filling station was his regular one.

Could it be that at that time, he would have been unsure whether Carol, during her interview, had included the petrol station visit if they had not in fact called there? It wouldn't have made sense if they hadn't purchased the petrol because the obtaining of the £2 loan from her dad was the reason (or excuse) they used for going back home early from the pub. This theory becomes even firmer when considering the fact that later consumption tests conducted on the vehicle cast considerable doubt as to whether any petrol was indeed purchased.

It was also then that Latham volunteered that he had forgotten something else about his movements. He told the officers that he had visited David Edwards, the jewellers to have his watch set and cleaned after they had left the dentists. It was the second time that he had been there and Carol had remained in the car.

Latham then became a little upset and commented that he should be at home with Carol. He asked who was in charge and after being told and the fact that he should be co-operating, stated that he would want an apology for being kept away from her.

There then followed a conversation about John's involvement with scrap metal and that John wanted him to go into business with him as he was bragging that he could invest thousands of pounds in what could be made. He commented that all he wanted to do was go abroad.

DS Griffiths then explained that as he was apparently the last person to see John alive, then if he hadn't committed the murder, then he should want to clear himself. He agreed and also agreed that he should have a medical examination to prove his innocence. This was already being arranged by myself and that interview by DS Griffiths and DC McIntosh was then concluded at 1.55am.

Carol Davies's 1st Interview - Continued

Now to return to where we had left Carol's interview for the purpose of introducing Danny McLaughlin and Phil Breakwell. She had described the history between herself and Latham, including the fact that Latham was eager to travel to South Africa in August, to obtain work.

So, they arrived at Danny McLaughlin's girlfriend's house, (where Danny had been living) at about 2pm to 2.35pm. The information adduced by her was contained in a witness statement formatted by DPW Gwyther, in Det. Inspector Herbert's presence.

The next step in her itinerary was that unlike Latham (surprise, surprise!) she recalled that they had stopped at The Minster Self Service petrol station where Latham delivered £2's worth of petrol to her car whilst she went to the office to pay for it. It was from there that they went to visit Danny McLaughlin. Danny's common law wife Lorraine Albutt and their three-year-old toddler were there, as was Lorraine's younger sister, Carol. She estimated that they were there for about twenty minutes, talking about the forthcoming darts match and drinking coffee.

It will become apparent later that visiting McLaughlin without prior arrangement was far from normal and in any event, McLaughlin would have already been aware that he would be playing in this darts match. Their visit was therefore entirely unnecessary.

From there, they went directly to the Kidderminster General Hospital concerning Doug's treatment for cancer. This was a surprise because in Latham's description, he called it "pains in the chest". We now have Carol stating that the visit concerned his cancer treatment. She stated that they were there for approximately 15 to 20 minutes and that he had been advised that if his pains persisted, then he should return to the hospital.

Carol then told the officers that they then drove to 64 Walter Nash Road (it is in fact number 63 Walter Nash Road) the home of their friends, Tom and Sheila Parry, concerning a car which Mr. Parry had for sale. It was following this last visit that they returned home to be met with the flurry of police activity.

WDC Gwyther then completed Carol's witness statement but it is interesting to note that in addition to Latham apparently forgetting to mention their return to the house to collect something, so did Carol also forget to inform the officers of that return visit when she was interviewed.

It was following his involvement in Carol's interview that Detective Inspector Herbert had an opportunity to acquaint himself with what had occurred in the interview of Doug Latham. It can be imagined how awkward it can become when two people are involved in the same joint enterprise and are interviewed by different people. There has to be a rapid exchange of information between the two sets of interviewers.

Douglas Latham - Medical Examination

In the meantime, prior to other interviews with Latham or Carol Davies, I was present at 1.55am the following morning, 28th January 1981 in the examination room at Kidderminster Police Station when Latham was medically examined by the Police Surgeon Dr. Johnson. When asked by the doctor, Latham informed him that he was unemployed but regularly helped John in his business of collecting scrap metal. No injuries were found on him but Dr. Johnson commented to him that his hands were extremely clean in relation to him collecting scrap metal.

The doctor also asked Latham if he had been sick recently and he replied to the effect that he had not been sick for the last few days.

I was to later conduct Latham's next interview but before then, Carol Davies was to again be interviewed by Detective Inspector Herbert and Det. Policewoman Gwyther and were then in possession of the above development concerning their return to 9 Clifton Road.

Carol Davies – Continuation of 1st Interview

This interview commenced at 2.30am on 28th January and it began with Det. Insp Herbert attempting to discover the health of both Carol and Latham. For herself, she stated that she had felt 'scared' at the dentists and that afterwards, she felt 'dopey', due to receiving the treatment.

It is interesting to note that in fact, she had seven teeth extracted that day and not eight as she had informed everyone she spoke to. She may well have been under a misapprehension but on the other hand, she may have exaggerated the number to add weight to her alleged, 'dopey' condition.

The importance of her condition and awareness cannot be overemphasised, because it was this drowsiness or 'dopiness' as she described it and attributed to herself, was the alleged cause of her not remembering some important facts.

Carol went on to explain that she saw no difference in Latham's appearance or behaviour during the day but because he felt sick, he went to the bathroom as soon as they had arrived at Danny McLaughlin's home. She explained that Latham had spent 5-10 minutes in the upstairs bathroom at Danny's, as opposed to using the downstairs toilet.

She could not remember if Latham said that he had been sick but Danny had joined him in the bathroom to see how he was.

Having failed to remember their returning to the house not long after leaving it, as soon as Det. Inspector Herbert mentioned this, and that he suggested to Carol that Latham could be responsible for her father's death, she immediately recalled the visit and that it was in order for him to recover his cigarettes. Most importantly, she stated that his return visit to the house took no longer than half a minute.

With only Latham and herself knowing that they had returned home, she did not, of course, have any option but to now include this re-visit to the house. Having had this put to her, she would have automatically realised that Latham would have included it in his version of their movements that day.

Assuming that they had committed the murder, it was, of course, imperative for them to provide identical stories if they had any chance to make their alibi work.

She said that she had remained in the car all of the time he was in the house and when he returned, she couldn't see any change in his appearance or demeanour. She completely discounted the suggestion that Latham could be responsible.

It was also put to her that she could be covering up for her boyfriend but again, she discounted that theory by forcefully saying, "DON'T BE MAD, HE'S ME FLAMING DAD, I WAS 'DOPEY' AT THE HOUSE".

She said that whilst she wasn't taking much notice, she couldn't remember seeing anyone in the vicinity of the house.

She was then questioned about her father's relationship with other people and she said that he was always falling out with people and that him being the Trade Union Representative at his work may have been a factor.

She maintained that there was no reason why Latham should have fallen out with her dad and that it wasn't he who borrowed money from him. She said that she normally borrowed, on average, £5 per week from him. Whilst she agreed that her father disliked the idea of both of them being on the dole, she was keen to suggest that it caused no aggravation between them.

It was most startling when she mentioned that the only area of aggravation in the household was between herself and her dad. She alleged that her father looked upon Doug as a son. This was very much in contradiction to information later revealed from other sources, when it was discovered that John despised Latham and had reduced himself to tears when discussing him and his relationship with his daughter, with other people.

Carol and her mother had both arrived at the police station much earlier. Betty had been waiting in the reception area to be joined by her daughter and Latham, to be released from assisting with the police's appreciation of the domestic situation and movements of the household members during that day.

However, although these persons were free to leave at any time following this interview and indeed, it was suggested to them that they did so, they both declined and stated that they wished instead to wait for Latham, before returning to their neighbours' house.

Medical Examination of Carol Davies

My presence at Latham's medical examination terminated with the ending of his examination, shortly before commencing my interview with Latham at 3.15am. At that time, Doctor Johnson commenced his medical examination of Carol. It was carried out with her consent and in the presence of WDC Gwyther.

Her condition was generally satisfactory though she was pale and slightly nervous. Her blood pressure and pulse were normal. Her clothes were removed and handed to WDC Gwyther for forensic examination. Blood samples were taken.

The Management of Personnel - PACE

It is as well to pause for thought here, concerning new legislation which came into effect as a result of the Police and Criminal Evidence Act, 1984, (PACE) which I have already mentioned. This was three years away.

Now it must also be remembered that all of the Detectives involved in this inquiry had been on duty since approximately 9am on the morning of Tuesday 27th January, 1981. These wouldn't just include the interviewing officers, but a whole host of officers were by now being tasked to man the 'Incident Room' and to make the ad hoc inquiries resulting from all ongoing external inquiries as well as that evolving from these interviews.

'Actions' amounting to a type of 'job sheet' would be compiled and issued, mainly by one person, in this case, Det. Chief Superintendent David Cole who, as the 'Senior Investigating Officer' (SIO), would have not been getting himself tangled up in interviews.

He would have been keeping an overall appreciation of the information emanating from all of them and ensuring that all aspects of the investigation were properly fed into the HOLMES system.

As mentioned before, this was over 40 years ago and although exact numbers cannot be remembered, there were bound to be about fifty officers involved and this might well have increased as time went on. I can recall two Divisional Heads of CID in the rank of Detective Chief Inspectors, (DCIs) being drafted in to 'manage' the handling of important information and people suddenly appearing on the stage, such as McLaughlin and Breakwell. These were Detective Chief Inspector Barrington (Barrie) Mayne and Detective Chief Inspector Keith Smith.

It was now getting well into the early hours of the day following the murder and it might well be appreciated that Carol Davies and Douglas Latham would inevitably be required to answer further questions. This was because, resulting from their early interviews, 'actions' would have been rolled out from them in addition to what was being learned from subsequent information received from all sources, not just from their subsequent interviews.

When considering that, it was obviously going to be necessary to interview the other people mentioned by them. McLaughlin and Breakwell would obviously head the queue.

It was also very much desirable that at the time when they were regarded as suspected of somehow being involved, it was essential to keep them from getting their heads together and also, making contact with those who had yet to be interviewed.

It was also obvious that myself and all others involved in this investigation from the start, would not be able to continue for very long, without gaining some sleep. But surely, the success of the investigation was bound to be compromised and the momentum upset, if those of us already employed in the interviews were to be substituted by others.

In addition, this wouldn't have been the first case to have been 'thrown out' of court because the suspects involved hadn't been afforded proper rest breaks, comfort and food etc. We had all missed going to bed that night of the 27th January 1981.

This was naturally a management issue which would have been far easier to have handled in the days prior to the Police and Criminal Evidence Act, which had not then been introduced.

Therefore, the point I wish to make in raising this is that under the new provisions of PACE, the police can only hold suspects for up to 24 hours before they have to charge them with a crime or release them. In serious cases like murder, 24 hours can be extended on application to a court, for periods of 36 and sometimes, 96 hours.

In this case, there were only two major suspects, with the possibility of others in the wings. We, who were currently engaged in the interviews from the start, would be running on adrenalin but, at some stage, we could be in danger of crashing into exhaustion.

In the proverbial 'old days', and we were now working in those old, 'Pre-PACE' days, things were a great deal different.

It was then possible to put all concerned, including the suspects, in effect, to 'sleep' in order to continue the processes after perhaps a shorter than normal sleep. That was comparatively easy to do but, of course, it wouldn't have been professional to have allowed Latham and Carol Davies to have got their heads together and so, with their permission, we needed to progress to the cautioning and arresting stage when the evidence permitted.

I wasn't the only detective to have been through this process a few times, and of course, the adrenalin rush will inevitably prevent, or drastically shorten, anything like a good sleep. So far as suspects are concerned, could anyone imagine that they were going to have a good sleep? I think not, as they would be going over events both as they actually happened and as they considered themselves, how best to portray what had happened, so as to paint the best picture they could, in order to save their necks.

So, with that intrusion, can any reader begin to understand how on earth a large inquiry would cope these days with a multitude of suspects, when having to keep their eyes open to the new requirements of PACE? This law was obviously made by people with good intentions, but who were without a clue as to what justice demanded.

The rights of suspects must, of course, be observed but goodness knows how such investigations are properly handled these days.

With all that to consider, plus the fashion of advertising the advantages of 'NO COMMENT' interviews on television, is it any wonder that the morale of officers involved in crime investigations has taken a nose dive, with officers said to be merely going through the motions of the interviews as we have all witnessed on TV?

10. The Reluctant Dancers

Having completed what was going to be the first of many long interviews with Douglas Latham and Carol Davies, it should become obvious to readers that, with both having mentioned that they had called on Danny McLaughlin and Phil Breakwell on that afternoon, 27th January, we would very quickly wish to see both of them. They were going to be very useful in either supporting what Latham and Carol had both said, or would this become a part of an elaborate, though simple alibi?

Apart from Latham not mentioning the visit to the petrol filling station, which Carol did, there was little difference between their stories and the filling station might well have been a slip of Latham's memory. However, the analogy with reluctant dancers comes to mind because whilst at first, McLaughlin and Breakwell wanted to get on that dancefloor, they later became analogous to those people at dances, often described as wallflowers. They wanted to get on the dance floor, but were reluctant to make any moves to get there.

However, these two showed all the eager signs of accepting their invitations; indeed, they quickly got up to dance but when the music started to play, one hadn't the nerve to continue to the floor and the other was stopped and returned to his seat, because the music had stopped playing.

So let us briefly describe their first steps in relation to them being briefly interviewed as witnesses by my colleagues, DCI Barrie Mayne and DCI Keith Smith.

In McLaughlin's case, he was actually seen on the same day as the murder and he made what was just over a two-page witness statement supporting Latham and Carol in saying that he was at his girlfriend's home at about 2.15pm to 2.30pm, when they both called unexpectedly. He became aware that Latham wanted to go upstairs to the bathroom as he felt sick.

He joined him and shortly after, they drank coffee in the living room and discussed the darts match to be played on the following evening. Doug seemed fine and he was playing with McLaughlin's little child.

McLaughlin gave a good description of what clothes both Latham and Carol were wearing and they left the flat to go to the hospital at about 3pm, to attend to Doug's chest pains.

Their conversation was indeed, exactly the same as that described by Latham and Carol.

McLaughlin's Arrest

However, it was well into the early hours of the following morning that Latham was again interviewed and it will be seen later that he willingly implicated McLaughlin in an enterprise involving the stealing of some telephone cable from Martley. It was, of course, normal and professional to ensure that our colleagues in the Major Incident Room were fed details of interviews as soon as possible, so that arrest plans could be formed and witnesses could be interviewed without delay.

In McLaughlin's case, Latham's disclosures meant he would need to be seen again and arrested over this and further interviewed. He was indeed invited to return to the police station with DCIs Mayne and Smith and after a short interview, he was arrested and detained in the cells. He had still not been open and frank about the role he had played and continued to try to protect Latham and pull the wool over our eyes.

In his words, it was when he was placed in the cells, that he realised that he was in a serious situation. He knew that he had not been involved in the killing, so had nothing to hide there. However, being arrested and placed in a cell, he began to realise that he was in trouble over conspiring with them, not to mention trying to pervert the course of justice. At this very early stage, he therefore decided that he would open up and tip the bean bag completely upside down to spill them all. And so, he asked to see the interviewing officers.

Unfortunately, DCIs Mayne and Smith were then engaged with other enquiries and he was told that someone would see him during the next day, 29th January. He had put himself in this situation, but just think what might have then been going through his mind. He wanted to talk but he couldn't. If I had been in his shoes, I wouldn't have slept much that night.

Although he knew that he had nothing to do with John's death, he had been shielding Latham and Carol by not telling the police all that he knew. He was a worried man.

It was then that in a statement under caution, he made a full and frank confession of what he knew. He described all of the background knowledge he had about John Davies and his daughter, Carol and how he had first met Latham in the pub when they talked about darts and football. It was ironic that he had been unaware that Carol was John Davies's daughter, because he had indeed, previously worked on the dustcarts with John.

It was after two or three meetings that Latham asked him if he wanted to earn some money to kill someone. This of course was a long, drawn-out conversation and made over two or more of their meetings. He got to learn that it was Caroline's dad who they wanted killed and that it would be done by shooting him. He had been taken to the house to go over the layout and to discuss various places where it could be done.

It is now that McLaughlin suggests that although he informed Latham that he would go along with his plans, he had no intentions of shooting anyone. He had been firmly under the impression that Latham had just been bragging and that it was just pub 'Big Talk'.

He also mentioned in his statement, their visit to Martley to rob an old lady who lived in a cottage which John had owned. It was in this cottage that he understood John had kept an unlicensed double-barrelled shotgun with which they could kill him. Whilst at the cottage, he also said that Doug had pointed out a few places where John could be ambushed.

However, the cottage was still occupied by the old lady tenant and so they decided to return after dark and burgle the unoccupied cottage next to it to get some goods to sell, as they were all broke at that time. This they did and the stolen property was sold in Worcester. His dividend of the proceeds amounted to a grand total of eight pounds.

McLaughlin then said that it was shortly after that he met Latham in the Bridge pub, when he told him of the plans to rob a bank in Worcester. John and Carol were also there and because Latham had told him that it would be just John and him in on this robbery, McLaughlin asked Doug to ask John if he could be included.

Doug told him that he doubted that, because he, McLaughlin and John had previously worked on the dustcarts together and John didn't like him.

However, a couple of days later, McLaughlin was approached by John himself who asked him if he could get some shooters for this bank robbery. Being the big 'I am' again, he told him that he thought he could. He explained however, that once again, he thought that this was just 'big talk'.

Their attempts to obtain weapons via a contact through a mutual friend, George Bettis, will be described later at the appropriate time. By this time, Phil Breakwell had also been recruited into the conspiracy and it was obvious that as far as was then known, McLaughlin was not intentionally holding back on any of the information he possessed.

Above all, McLaughlin fully described what had happened when he joined Latham in his girlfriend's bathroom and he emphasised that all this had now frightened him and that he had never intended to go along with what Latham had planned, nor had he believed that Latham would.

It will be seen later, that McLaughlin's involvement in court proceedings was to take an extraordinary turn and although he had openly shared what he knew, on 18th February, he was to make a further witness statement which would embrace the first witness statement and then the whole of the statement referred to above which was made as a suspect, under caution. I recorded his statement which was the longest one I had ever recorded. It was 36 pages in length and was taken over two days.

Philip Robert Breakwell

With various interview teams all being very busy during the first two days, Phil Breakwell was left to be the last of the four alleged conspirators to be interviewed. It was apposite that this was the case, because he was even further away from the core of the action than were Latham, Carol and McLaughlin.

Breakwell was seen on the day following the murder, Wednesday, 28th January 1981. He had in fact, only arrived home from his tour as a soldier in Münster, Germany, exactly two weeks prior to the murder being committed.

In that short space of time, he had been drawn into meeting Doug and Carol and had only recognised her as a girl who had attended the same senior school as he had. He had never met Latham.

He hadn't been there for the proverbial five minutes before he had been recruited to play darts for The Bridge Inn pub's darts team in an 'away' match at the 'Live and Let Live' pub at Fernhill Heath, Worcester.

It was there, that he had been drawn into a conspiracy to murder someone and had volunteered to be the driver of the stolen 'getaway' car after the shooting.

This had been an amazing two-week period in the life of Philip Breakwell. He had been in Germany, he had returned home, he had met two people he had not known before, he had been wearing a 'T' shirt with the motif, **'DON'T MESS WITH THE SAS'** thereon, which had attracted the attention of Doug Latham. Remarkably, all this had combined as essential ingredients to him becoming involved in a conspiracy to murder. It was certainly an unbelievable couple of weeks. Maybe he had brought it upon himself, by trying to portray himself as a member of the SAS Regiment.

It had been both Latham and McLaughlin who broached the subject with him but it was on the following Friday, 16th January, only three days into his home leave, that Latham fully propositioned him to shoot Carol's father. He thought Latham was joking and even after Latham had said that it would be worth £3,000 for three shots, he still did not believe him and thought that it was just 'Big Talk'.

Two nights later, Breakwell said that he met up with Latham and Carol again at the Bridge Inn and that Latham was openly talking about shooting Carol's dad in her presence and hearing. However, again, he thought that this was just 'Big Talk' and that he was only joking.

Breakwell's statement also included details of the trip over to Worcester to meet someone who could supply the weapons required. Ironically, he said that both Latham and McLaughlin were wearing suits to make them look a little more like the part of gangsters attempting to get hold of guns. This was the attempt that went wrong and will be described in full, later.

Breakwell also included the reconnoitre around Clifton Road, so that Latham and Carol could plan his escape from the area after the shooting. It was after that when he started to believe that what they had been discussing was more than 'Big Talk' and so he sought to extricate himself from this mess. To do so, he came up with a story about falling down the stairs and pretended   injured his knees which would preclude him from driving the 'getaway' car.

The next thing he knew was seeing the news about the murder on TV. He had been three days away from when the murder had taken place. If firearms had been available, he had been so close to taking part in murdering John.

At this time, although there was much more work to be done, we were quite happy that we had rounded off the case with Latham actually causing John's death and with him, Carol and the two conspirators well and truly cooked for conspiring to kill him. The only doubt we were to continue being curious about, was whether Carol was present in the house when Latham did the killing. Although not critical, the other doubt centred on whether their return to the house after they had left was indeed factual.

There were, however, other interviews to take place.

11. Douglas Latham – 2nd Interview

Readers must realise that by including the arrests and interviews of McLaughlin and Breakwell above, we have leapfrogged over the progress we had made up to the completion of Latham and Carol's first interviews and that although the weight of suspicion was growing heavier, no arrests had then been made.

My next job was to interview Latham immediately following his medical examination at which I was present. The interview commenced at 3.15am on 28th January and I was accompanied by Detective Chief Inspector Ian Bullock and Detective Sergeant Richard Griffiths, who recorded notes of the interview.

It was at that point that I knew that Latham was certainly not going to be leaving the police station as a free man and probably not for a very long time. He had now fallen into the category of being a suspect, whether it was for murder or conspiracy to murder. This was about the time when the Judges' Rules dictated that persons in his position should be cautioned that they weren't obliged to say anything unless they wished to do so, but what they said, would be taken down in writing and may be given in evidence.

And so, I explained the nature of the 'caution' to him and went through what it meant. He had been through this procedure before but there was no way that I was going to compromise our situation and I recited it to him in addition to fully explaining it to him.

He was not going to try to explain away some of the pointers which at that time indicated that he might well be involved. He was thought then to have gone to a lot of trouble planning a long and involved alibi and without trying to wriggle through the cracks, he would have known that he was doomed.

But before we reached his 'wriggling' situation, I went through the domestic situation at 9 Clifton Road.

This would have set him off talking as there could be nothing contentious for him to say apart from perhaps about his relationship with John. If, after chatting about nothing in dispute, he was to suddenly refuse to answer more tricky questions, then inferences of guilt may be drawn. Or could they?

I say this because one of my pet subjects in crime investigations and the law, is that the current guidance dictating the processes of justice dictate that jurors must not take any such inferences of guilt from suspects who refuse to answer police questions. This is because they are only acting within their rights of silence.

My issue is that they should be warned that whilst they need not answer questions, those investigating crimes and jurors at trials may take into consideration whatever inferences they draw from that decision by suspects who elect to make no comment to questions they are asked.

We were aware that John was very protective of his daughter and detested Latham. He really didn't want him living under the same roof.

But Latham also knew that John was dead and couldn't contradict what he was now about to say.

However, Latham may not have known then (nor did we until later) that we would learn that during the morning of 15th November 1980, 10 weeks prior to his murder, John had made a visit to Kidderminster Police Station, where he spoke to PC Terence Law. The purpose of his visit was that he wanted to know how he could prevent his daughter, Carol from going out with Latham.

He was advised that his daughter was over 21 and of course, this was not a police matter. However, he was told that he could visit a solicitor with a view to obtaining an injunction to stop Latham from entering his house, if that was what he wished.

We were also to discover that at about this time (about three weeks before Christmas) that John had spoken to a close work colleague of his, a Michael Keechan. It was during the investigation that he informed the police that John had broken down in tears during a conversation with him, telling Mr. Keechan that he didn't like his daughter going out with Latham who he referred to as 'a tramp'.

John told him that he didn't trust him and that Latham wanted to take his daughter away to South Africa. He said that Latham and Carol had tried to get £7,000 out of him to buy a tourer vehicle to travel there. He said that he wouldn't give them seven pence, let alone £7,000. Mr Keechan said that he had never seen John in such a state before, it was so unusual.

In addition, Mr Stan Burley, who lived directly opposite to the Davies family, stated that a month or two before that Christmas, John confided in him about the same subject. He also said that John had tears in his eyes about his daughter and her lazy boyfriend wanting to emigrate to South Africa.

All this was, of course, to be in direct contrast to Carol stating that it was John's idea that Latham move in with the family and that he treated him like a son. It also demonstrates how important it is to record the background situation before anyone, let alone a suspect, is questioned about such matters. However, back to the interview. Latham explained that he was to use the small 'box' room to sleep alone as John was against him sleeping with Carol.

He explained that John was worried about what the neighbours would say and in fact, they had 'words' about the situation, though it wasn't a 'heated' argument. Perhaps displaying some of his boastful characteristics, he just had to add that this did not stop his sexual relationship with Carol when John was not in the house or when he was asleep.

He said that the relationship between Carol and her father was very good. Carol would discuss things with him more so than with her mother. He gave as an example the fact that John told Carol that the reason why he had been suspended from work was that he had fallen down because he was drunk and not because he had slipped on ice, as he had told his wife and his bosses at work. He also mentioned that a particular work colleague, John's Inspector, whose name he did not know, was trying to get him the sack over this incident.

He continued by volunteering that he had only borrowed a small amount off John on one occasion to buy a car and that he had repaid him, all but for £10. Although amounts were not discussed, he said that whilst he had no savings in this country, he did so in Iran.

When asked if he knew why anyone would want to enter the house and kill John, he mentioned three possibilities of motive. He said that it was common knowledge that John always carried large amounts of money on his person. Also, there were the 'Ups and Downs' at work and lately, they had been receiving funny phone calls: when he and Carol had answered the phone, the line went dead.

He particularly mentioned a telephone call when the caller asked for Arthur John Davies and not the name he was always known by, 'John' Davies. On this occasion, the caller had asked that John be informed that his houses were ready for John to look at. The houses were apparently in Birmingham but when John was told of the message, he denied knowing anything about houses in Birmingham. However, some days later, he mentioned that it was best to invest in property. Latham clearly believed to the contrary.

He then explained the amounts of money he had witnessed John carrying and then expanded on what he knew of John's scrap metal business and that on one occasion he saw that he had about £200 - £400 in his wallet. It was then that Latham spoke of John's intention to steal some copper wire from some 'tatters' (gypsy type scrap collectors) at Martley.

The metal in question would be worth about £7-800 and was in the area where John was raised in his earlier years. He said that John had originally asked him to go with him to steal it but that later, John told both Carol and himself that it had already gone.

This, of course, was quite a significant statement to make and provides an insight into the social atmosphere of the house and the 'open' relationships between these three. Here we have a father talking to his daughter and her prospective husband about quite a serious case of theft, as if it was some everyday item being read from a newspaper.

I then reflected again on the events of what was now, 'yesterday' the day of the murder. Again, he went through the events, just as he had done as earlier described. However, he said that John had enjoyed his work with the new team he had been assigned to because they were finishing earlier than his old team.

The 26th January was indeed, John's first day back to work as an ordinary 'dustman' and not the chargehand driver he had been previously.

He had in effect, been demoted after he had been put on gardening leave by his bosses following their discipline enquiry. This period had been referred to by all concerned as a 'holiday'.

Latham described again about the leaving of the back door key which was on Carol's car keyring. The reason, he described, was because John had commented that he was going out to meet someone, but he did not say who he was meeting.

Whether in fact John did leave the house that afternoon is a moot question. The only importance that can be attributed to the answer is whether or not the description about leaving the key with John to facilitate him leaving and then returning to their home before Latham and Carol returned, was true or not.

In that context, evidence was taken from the garage proprietor who John used to repair his vehicles. This was Mr Michael Gosling, who stated that he was visited by John at his business premises at "about lunchtime" on the day of his murder. However, he had missed lunch that day and he was not certain of the time. He suggested it was between 1pm and 2.30pm or so he thought. He further stated that the purpose of his visit was to pay an outstanding debt of £5.16.

Due to the passage of time and the fact that I would not be in court if and when Mr Gosling was called to give evidence, I cannot now recall whether indeed, he gave this evidence. It seems unlikely that having owed this small sum for some time, John would have made a special trip to pay it. In any event, the question is perhaps inconsequential to the outcome of the trial.

The rest of the events included the driving of Carol to the dentists and him visiting the jewellers to have his watch looked at. There was no deviation here from his previous account, including their visit to the Bridge Inn where he spoke to the landlord and his wife and Phil Breakwell, the soldier on home leave. He stated that he had drunk at least three or four pints of beer and was happy, but he knew what he was doing and was not drunk.

When asked about his health, he explained that he hadn't felt well for two days, however, they left the pub and arrived home at about two o'clock.

He said that he was broke and because of that, he was intending to then stay at home. However, he realised that he wanted to see Danny McLaughlin about the darts match and after they arrived home, Carol borrowed the £2 off her dad to get some petrol for the car. He had £10 upstairs but he wanted to keep that so that they could go back to the pub later on. His wallet was later found to indeed contain £11.

At that time, John was lying on the settee talking to Carol about her dental treatment. Having now already stated that he returned to the house a short time after leaving it, but had forgotten to previously mention it, he now readily remembered it and stated that he had "forgotten his fags". He parked the car outside behind John's pick-up vehicle and, after picking up his cigarettes, left the house about thirty seconds later.

We had not made Latham aware that we had discovered traces of blood in the upstairs bathroom, and so, when detailing his movements about the house after they arrived there from the pub, what would have appeared to have been an incongruous question, was indeed, a very important one. When asked if he went upstairs at that time, it was our good fortune that he said that he hadn't and that they were only there for about 10 to 15 minutes and left again at around 2.15pm.

It was, of course, this return trip to the house made shortly after they had left it, which was conveniently forgotten by both Carol and Latham, that had started the bells of suspicion to ring more loudly. The whole trip being forgotten by one of them is one thing, but the coincidental forgetting by both of them, is another.

However, up until this point, readers will realise that the police are now at that stage, where the pair have both provided their full accounts about where they went and what they did. That is not to say that their accounts were believed, but more importantly, that is their version of events which have, up to this point, not been questioned or challenged in any way.

It was fundamentally important to allow those being interviewed the freedom to complete their version of events without interruption. The structuring of future interviews would be built on their versions and hopefully, some loopholes would appear in what they said.

This tactic isn't a question of being clever, its pure common sense, but so often, the temptation to challenge at too early a stage is so strong that one can so easily fall into that trap, as I had obviously done when Phil Paton had been supervising my early attempts at being 'Sherlock Holmes' at Hereford.

So now is the time when the right questions can be asked. Contrary to what often is viewed on TV, we don't want to start pointing the finger just yet: well, maybe an indication in the tone of voice will do here, but of course not all interviewees have the same sorts of responses.

And so, with regard to the need to go back to the house for forgotten cigarettes, I questioned the fact by asking why he couldn't simply buy another packet. His response was that he didn't want to spend money at that time as he wanted to spend it in the pub later on.

Anyway, on his return to the house, he said that although the cigarettes were on the mantelpiece above the fire which John was in front of, he said that he didn't notice what he was doing. John was still lying on the settee and all he said to him was that he had returned for his "fags". He did not hear any answer from him.

When questioned about the timings of his visit, he suggested that it was about two minutes after they first left and that he was at the house for only about a minute on his second visit. He said that they then drove to the Minster Filling Station, but that he couldn't remember the sequence of events there, concerning who it was that actually paid for the £2 worth of petrol in the office. As that had happened less than 24 hours ago, his uncertainty about who had gone to the office to pay for the petrol was in itself, very questionable.

He then responded to questions by saying that they went straight to Danny's and although he had consumed three or four pints, he only went to the toilet when they arrived there. He explained that the premises were Danny's girlfriend's and that Danny was decorating, but he thought that they drank coffee and were only there for about an hour.

Whilst no positive evidence could pinpoint the exact time of John's death, events were indicating that it had happened around the time of Carol and Latham's presence at the scene. It was therefore extremely important to probe their movements over every second around that time.

To that end, the questions asked resulted in him stating that he went to the upstairs toilet and that Danny followed him up there, because he had been told by Carol that he wasn't feeling "too good".

I said, "How did he know that, you were upstairs". He responded by saying that he heard Carol telling Danny that, as they entered the premises. He told me that he said that he wanted to go to the toilet as he was feeling 'queasy' or something similar and that he "had a slash" and washed his hands and that he was only in the toilet for about five minutes.

On returning to the living room, he said that they had a coffee and played with Danny's child, leaving there at about 3.30pm to call on Phil Breakwell. However, because he wasn't feeling well, he decided to go to the hospital where only the day before, he had received an ECG examination and had been prescribed some distalgesic tablets.

He said that, on this occasion, he was seen by a 'coloured' doctor who informed him that his heart was in good condition and that he should continue to take the tablets and to make an appointment to see his GP.

So having left the hospital, they drove to Claughton Street, to see Phil Breakwell, as was first intended. However, on this occasion, he said that he could not remember if calling on Breakwell was before or after the hospital visit. He did explain that the reason for wanting to see him was for him to give a message to the Licensee of the Bridge Inn, to say that he couldn't go out on that Tuesday evening "because he was broke".

Readers will be aware that Latham had previously spoken of not wanting to spend too much money on that Tuesday lunchtime because he wanted to keep the £10, which he declared that he had 'upstairs' due to the fact that he wanted to spend it in the pub on that Tuesday evening. It was also the fact that there was a telephone in the Davies household and no reason why such a trivial message needed to have been given by a third-party, when all he had to do was pick up the phone.

It may well have been the case that this message was more important than we might have believed, because Latham was casually employed behind the bar by this Alan, if and when they were extra busy, but that did not discount the obvious fact that he could simply give him a quick telephone call.

However, such a trivial reason for looking up Phillip Breakwell didn't carry much weight for Latham's defence and, of course, had Latham been responsible for John Davies's death, he had already been to the home of a possible fellow conspirator and Breakwell was possibly, at that time, viewed as another.

The feeling of the investigators at that time was that Latham had accomplished his objective of killing John and now he wanted to tell the others whom he had drawn into such a plan that the deed had been done. He had the 'bragging rights' and as we now know, bragging rights among them, even depended on life or death to some of them.

In addition to building an alibi for themselves, the other possible motive for making these bizarre visits might well have included the fact that they would not want to go home and discover the body themselves. That would have required talking themselves out of committing the murder when they had arrived. They needed to ensure that Carol's mother Betty had got home before they did.

So, we have strayed from what Carol had earlier described as a normal day for the two of them and now have a catalogue of visits paid by her and Latham on the very day that her father is murdered.

The dentist, the watch repair, the Bridge Inn, back home, the petrol station, Danny McLaughlin home, the hospital, Phil Breakwell's home and finally, we were to learn that prior to arriving back home after John's body had been discovered, they had visited yet another associate of theirs, a Mrs Sheila Parry.

This Parry family lived just around the corner from Clifton Road, in Walter Nash Road. Mrs Parry had known Latham since he was a boy, as her first husband was a friend of Latham's grandfather.

According to Latham, the purpose of the visit was for him to enquire if Mrs Parry's husband Tom had sold a car which he was trying to sell recently. This was a Ford Zodiac which had been parked outside on the verge for some time whilst it was for sale. The vehicle had already been sold and Mr. Parry states that Latham would have known that in any event, as it had been missing from its parking place for some time.

Latham states that he first saw the Parrys' daughter who confirmed that the car had been sold. Nevertheless, they stayed for about half an hour before returning to their home at Clifton Road, just two tenths of a mile away. Only to be met by the flurry of activity following the discovery of John's murder.

I put it to Latham that what he had been doing was trying to compile an alibi for his movements that day. His response was, "I often go visiting people for something to do. I don't like being stuck in the house."

I also suggested to Latham that, if he had been involved in the murder, there was every chance that John's blood would be found on his clothes. He responded that that was impossible, because he hadn't been involved in John's murder.

The tempo of the interview was gradually being increased and it wasn't long before I dropped the scenario on his toes, I said, "The situation is, that whoever killed John would have known that he was at home."

I said, "They almost certainly knew he would be alone, were almost certainly known to him and knew they could gain access to the house through a door which would be open. What's more, they would need to not disturb the dogs to gain access. All this fits you. Who else would you know who had that knowledge and who would have a reason for killing him?

Latham almost immediately responded with – **"Bill Sprague – Stourport"**.

The sudden uttering of a name we had yet to hear from anyone's lips was strange enough and I have to say that I was thrown back on my heels. One of the reasons why this sudden utterance had been made could well have been that he had painted himself into a corner.

His response as to why? was again bizarre. He suggested that John had asked him if he could get some automatic pistols for doing a bank job and that his response was" No Chance". He then continued by saying that John had told him that he could get them from a person at Stourport – and then came the name, 'Bill Sprague'.

When asked who this Bill Sprague was, he said that he had heard his name and that he came from Stourport and he thought that he was in some way connected with engineering.

The subject of a bank robbery was, of course, completely fresh territory and one wonders whether this was the start of a plausible reason leading to a motive for the murder, or whether it was Latham taking on the mantle of a 'Walter Mitty' character in a desperate attempt to extricate himself from that 'painted in' corner.

He went on to say how John had told him that he was going to do a bank job because, "If you're going to do anything, you might as well do something that is worthwhile. Once it starts, there is no stopping, there's nobody giving up, it will be a shoot-out until the end. Either we get away or not."

With the obvious surprise that such a plan was now hoisted into the equation of John's death, I asked him how these guns would be paid for. This was when Latham again mentioned the ton of copper that John was planning to steal from the gypsies at Martley.

At my invitation, he then described the 'bank job' as involving the kidnapping of the bank manager's wife and any children they had and they would be taken in a stolen car just outside the bank. The manager would be taken to a window to be shown his wife and children in the stolen car.

He described the location of the bank and that it would involve another stolen car parked about a mile from the bank and five people, including John and himself. He was unaware as to the identity of the others. The bank manager would need to pay up or his wife and children would be killed. He would also be warned not to raise the alarm until two hours had elapsed.

When asked why that would all lead to Sprague killing John, he responded with "No Idea".

Our conversation led on to the scrap copper wire at Martley. Because Carol and her family once lived in that area, he, Latham, discussed it with Carol and they both went to view the wire. Latham had already told us that John mentioned stealing the wire, but had since discovered that it was gone. It apparently had not gone because Latham now stated that he and Carol had subsequently viewed it and that some of it was GPO cable. Latham said that they hadn't told John that they had viewed it.

This then led us to suspect the possibility that Latham may have orchestrated the theft of this wire himself, without telling John anything about it. This was put to him but of course he denied doing that. It was further put to him that if they had stolen it, John's death might have been as a result of him finding this out. This too, was denied.

This interview had obviously opened up the enquiry and there were many 'actions' which would be forthcoming as a result. The resistance to John losing his daughter to Latham's plans to emigrate to South Africa with her was always, on the face of it, a weak reason to go and kill him.

We were now treading into other waters and some kind of 'fallout' among thieves was a possibility. The understanding of any motive for killing someone is obviously very important and we would need to know.

The irony surrounding the alleged theft of the copper wire was that in fact it was never stolen at all. Its owner was traced and we were to learn that it was he who burnt the covering off the cable and indeed took it to the same dealer at Brierley Hill as John frequently used.

This interview concluded at 7.15am when DS Griffiths read over each question and answer he had noted of our conversation. Latham also read them as they were dictated to him. He signed each one and at the foot of each page.

The procedures of Latham writing up an endorsement at the end of the notes and for myself, DCI Ian Bullock and Det. Sgt Griffiths also signing them, took us up to the end of that session with Latham and by now, at 8am I said to him: -

> *You have come here of your own free will in connection with the death of Carol's father. During this interview, you have involved yourself in a conspiracy to rob and to steal metal. You are now under arrest and will remain here whilst I continue the enquiry. I will no doubt see you again.*

He was then cautioned and taken to the cells by DS Griffiths whilst DCI Bullock and myself briefed the Senior Investigating Officer, Detective Chief Superintendent Cole and handed the notes taken to him.

12. Carol Davies - 2nd Interview

At 9.30am on 28th January, the day following the murder, DCI Bullock and myself commenced a further interview with Carol Davies whilst Det. Insp. Herbert took over the writing of the notes. She had volunteered to stay at the police station in the hope of Latham being released. One can, however, consider now that as this murder was turning out to be a joint enterprise with Latham, she would have been more than keen to have been with him because she knew full well that if their accounts didn't match, then they would be in trouble.

The other consideration about the investigation was that the three of us were now into our second full day without sleep. A decision had to be made as to whether we should continue with this interview or hand over to others. You can bet that neither of us even hinted that we wanted to hand it over. The interview with Latham had just broken open fresh lines of enquiry and we knew exactly what we wanted to put to Carol.

Whilst not yet implicated in the actual murder, there was a feeling that she might open up even further than Latham, especially as he had now implicated her in the other criminal matters he had disclosed. Handing over to others would have involved them having to catch up with exactly what had occurred beforehand, so, on we pressed.

I opened up by explaining that I wanted to speak to her about her father's association with members of the criminal fraternity.

She then spoke of people whom John dealt with concerning stolen property, in particular named persons, and being offered stolen brass, but said that he didn't buy it. He would buy stolen 'stuff' "if he thought he could get away with it" was her response. When asked if there was any particular criminal activity he was currently engaged in, she replied "Yes, when he was drunk three or four weeks ago, he went on about getting some guns for a job, he didn't say what job." I pressed her into realising that we were probably already aware of the circumstances. How else would we know and why were we asking these questions?

As if the penny had dropped, she then said, *"Oh, he's told you about the bank robbery?"*

So, here was an excellent indication of the affinity between herself and Latham. She had proved that she would cover for him so long as she could. So, if she is willingly seeking to hide Latham's part to play in this so-called 'Bank Robbery', and without expressing any remorse whatsoever about her father's death, that surely exemplifies who she would rather protect; her boyfriend or her deceased father? It surely also is an indication of her possible involvement with Latham.

> After asking, "What was it all about?" She said, *"A bank, he asked Doug if he wanted to be in, I don't know where the guns were coming from. He'd had some trouble at work and he told me he was going away for a few days to rob a bank. A couple of days later, he said he wanted four blokes' He was going to kidnap the bank manager's family. He wanted Doug to spread it around. Doug mentioned it to Danny McLaughlin and Phil Breakwell. He said he wanted to do it out of the area. I don't think Doug took it serious; he thought dad would back out. Dad was supposed to be getting the guns.*

Carol went on to describe a meeting at the Council depot where John worked. She said that her dad wanted to meet Danny there, so they drove Danny there. This would be during the week before John's death. Phil Breakwell was also in the car and Danny and her dad had had a row. She explained that her dad was the one who was going to finance the job and that was all she knew.

Carol went on to identify persons she knew who had sold her dad stolen property and the fact that he had a safety deposit box in a Bewdley bank. She recalled him buying some stolen gold sovereigns and these had been in it, some of which he had made up into rings. She also named a shoplifter and many various gypsies who had sold him scrap metal.

Carol also described what she said she knew about the idea to steal the copper wire at Martley, but that someone had disposed of it before they could steal it.

She said that she had seen it and it was worth about £800, which would fund the guns that they wanted for the bank robbery.

We then turned to the source from where the guns were going to be supplied and she said it would be -

> *"Some George from Wrexham in the SAS was going to get them. Dad spoke to Danny in the Bridge. Danny said that dad could have them to try for nothing but if he wanted to keep them, he'd have to pay £100. Another George from Sion Hill put Danny onto this bloke from Wrexham. Anyway, the bloke didn't turn up. Doug was to put £50 down and Dad £50. Doug left some money for expenses."*

Carol continued to answer peripheral questions about this arrangement but of course, she had by now, possibly implicated herself in the commission or attempted commission of criminal offences which is why I formally cautioned her.

Whilst stating that she understood, she responded by saying, "Yes, it's nothing to do with me. I just know what's going on. I've done nothing".

She went on to say that the bank to be robbed was in Worcester, also that her father was a man of regular habits and most people would know what time he got home and that he had a sleep in the afternoon. She repeated what she had already told Detective Inspector Herbert earlier, that Doug was no more than 30 seconds in the house when he returned to pick up his cigarettes. She remained in the car and wasn't aware that anyone would have seen her waiting for Doug, although Mr and Mrs Burley, across the road, didn't miss much as they looked out for each other's houses.

She repeated the fact that several persons used to call at the house selling scrap but she was unaware if any of them had fallen out with her father. Other matters concerning her father's habits were then discussed. When asked if she was aware of his finances, she said that her parents had a joint account containing about £3-4,000. She said that she thought her father had small amounts at the T.S.B. at Kidderminster and at the Bank of Scotland.

She was under the impression that her father owned a cottage and some land at Shelsley Beauchamp, but that when she and Doug were caught poaching, the policeman told her that he didn't own the land any more. She said that they were poaching with a gun borrowed from a Steve Morris, but that Doug had told the police it was his because Morris didn't have a gun licence.

Steve Morris was interviewed and confirmed that he had loaned his single-barrel 12-bore shotgun to Latham. Latham, Carol, McLaughlin and Phil Breakwell weren't particular friends of his but casual acquaintances at the Bridge Inn. He had seen them talking together and when anyone approached them, they stopped talking as if they didn't want to be overheard.

In answer to other questions, she confirmed that her dad didn't like Danny McLaughlin and that they rowed at the depot over the money required for the guns. She denied that she would be involved in the bank robbery. It was her dad's idea when he almost lost his job.

She later explained that at first, Danny said that the guns would be free on approval, but then wanted some money to put down as a deposit. Her dad refused to pay him any money and this was what the row was all about.

Enquiries at his depot revealed that her comments concerning her dad losing his job were a reference to him being interviewed at work over two complaints of him being drunk during his morning's dustcart round. He had been a chargehand driver, a supervisor of his team and he tried to cover up his drunkenness by saying that he had taken some 'Headex' tablets and had fallen on some ice. The letter he received from the council indicated that he wasn't fully believed but that he would be taken off his driving and supervisory responsibilities, which meant a drop in pay. He had returned to work as a dustman on the day prior to his murder.

The interview terminated at 10.45am but Carol said that she would not leave the police station until her boyfriend was allowed to leave with her. By this time, she had been told that Latham would be required to be further interviewed. He had, of course, been arrested and medically examined and his clothes had been taken for forensic examination but he had not been charged with any offence.

Carol was not under arrest at that time but it very much suited the investigation team that she was at hand. She was therefore permitted to wait inside the police station.

13. – Douglas Latham - 3rd Interview. – 'A chink of light?'

It was important that once again, those present at Carol's 2nd interview, were immediately involved in a 'huddle' with the other senior investigating officers involved in the 'wider' enquiries. The left hand must know what the right hand is doing.

Our requirement now was to continue with interviewing Latham and if necessary, Carol Davies, but we now had another priority in that McLaughlin and Breakwell must be seen urgently.

Both had at least been included in some conspiracy to be involved in either the murder, the bank robbery, or both. My colleagues, Ian Bullock and Peter Herbert, could not afford to lose our grip on interviewing Carol Davies and Latham. We had not slept for a long time but we were still being driven on adrenalin. We all agreed that we were fine for continuing with these two prime suspects.

My memory has faded but if it had not already been agreed that the two Detective Chief Inspectors previously mentioned, Barrie Mayne and Keith Smith be employed in the McLaughlin and Breakwell direction, then they most certainly would have been now.

And so, at 12.35pm on that same day, 28th January, again together with Det. Ch. Insp. Bullock, we interviewed Douglas Latham. Detective Inspector Herbert took the notes.

Latham would have been sitting in his cell for some time, fully aware that whilst he may have been the leader of a conspiracy with Carol, McLaughlin and Breakwell, he was now separated from them. Whatever he had or had not done, Carol had been with him at all times with the possible exception of when he returned for that brief period, ostensibly to pick up his cigarettes. So, he would have naturally been very aware that the other three would have been interviewed at some stage or other.

But what would they say? He would not have been normal if he had not tossed around in his head what he would say in answer to whatever beans they may have spilled. To say nothing would only cast the shadow of suspicion further over his head. But what if only one or two of the three had decided to clear their own name(s)? His head must have been in turmoil.

His only advantage here was that he would know far more than us about how much influence he had over Carol. After all, she had been a loving daughter who was idolised by her father at least. She had by now cast aside all that past life and there was obviously nothing going to stand in her way of fleeing off to South Africa with this braggart, despite her father's wishes. She had already proved to us that she was a very hard nut to crack and, on reflection, we may have underestimated her loyalty to her boyfriend, Doug.

So, what would his problems be? He had to rely on the unknown fact as to what, if anything, we had been told by them. So, knowing what we did know, it would be interesting to ascertain what he would tell us without being prompted by questions. Would he change his story immediately? That was a possibility, but it would be more likely that he would wait to see what was put to him. The problem with that strategy was that it might well go against him if he were to amend his version of events when pressed.

So, the first statement I made to him after reminding him of the caution was that he had now had time by himself to think over the previous day's events. Had he missed out anything, or was there anything else he wanted to tell us?

His reaction was that he didn't know what I meant. Here we go, he would be fishing and so I threw him a little bait. I said, "Does the name 'George' mean anything to you? This question would have instantly registered to him that we knew of George Bainbridge and/or the other George (Bettis) from Sion Hill.

He said, "That George, yes, a bloke from Worcester. I met him in a café at Worcester under a railway bridge".

His attitude in not volunteering any further information was clear by his pause after answering. One would expect there to be a reason for this meeting, but nothing passed his lips. So I said, "What was that all about?"

He replied, "I went there with Danny and Phil. I wanted to see him. George Bainbridge his name was, to get two shotguns. He wanted a pony. I told him I hadn't got £25 cash. I told John who said 'no cash' so I said I'd give him £25 of my own money

"I went down the next day but he didn't turn up."

Having prompted him about how he knew this George Bainbridge, he had told us that another George - an ex-SAS man, from Sion Hill, Kidderminster - knew how to get guns. He said that he was given an address and was directed from there to the café. He said, "He was a bit of a nut. The first words he said to me was, "I could kill you."

He continued, again after being prompted and said that he asked what we wanted the guns for and that he told him that it was for a 'blagging' (Robbery). He said that this George told him to see him during the following day at George's house in Sion Hill. He later told the George at Sion Hill to give him a call when he arrived.

After asking him what he had given the George in Sion Hill for arranging this, he said, "Nothing. If it went alright, I'd drop him a penny". He also indicated that Phil wouldn't do a bank job and that he was returning to Germany soon to rejoin his regiment. Among our questioning, he also said the following: -

1. He didn't mention this during his previous interview because Bainbridge was a 'nutter' anyway.

2. There was no chance that he would be taking part in the robbery. He would have some money out of it but he wouldn't be taking part.

3. John wouldn't put up the money because Danny had told him that they could have them on account, for nothing.

4. It was when they went to the Council depot to discuss this with John that he and Danny argued about the situation.

5. Neither George Bainbridge nor the George from Sion Hill would know where John lived.

6. When he visited Danny on the previous day, nothing was discussed with him other than the darts match.

It was then that I said, "I can't accept that!"

If one places themself in Latham's shoes, I suspect that this comment, 'I can't accept that' was the trigger that caused him to believe that Danny had spilled the beans. What else in his mind, would make him believe that I couldn't accept what he had told me? The following questions and answers are therefore important and so I will repeat them here in the first person. For this remainder of the questions and answers session, his responses are in bold print.

So, in answer to my saying, "I can't accept that" He said, **"Purchasing the weapons I suppose".**

I said, "Go on".

He replied, **"I felt a bit queasy and went upstairs, he said, 'where have you been lately?" I asked him if there had been any development about buying the weapons. We were talking about weapons, about banks, about doing a blag. I asked him if he had done anything about it. He answered 'No'. I washed my hands and went down stairs."**

I said, "Come on, what else was said, you're stalling?"

It was then that he responded with an unbelievable answer and I think that it was an indication of him now believing that McLaughlin had indeed told the truth. He would have gained that belief from these questions. His response to my suggestion that he was stalling was – **"Yes, I am".**

I said, "Well?"

He replied, **"Somebody was going to do John. I know who the ones who would be responsible".**

He remained silent, so I told him that I thought he was trying to make up some time so he could think of the answers to my questions. I again urged him to continue.

His next response was even more surprising. He said,

"I turned around and told Danny he'd been done".

Again, he paused and I said, "How did you know that?"

He then banged his fist on the desk and raised his voice. His eyes rolled and he shouted -

"Alright, I found the fucking body, I could see his head was caved in. I went in and picked up my fags and saw him. I was probably there for five minutes. I nearly shit myself."

Although there was no pause in my response, I had felt that he was now sure that Danny had spilled the beans. The longer he was to stall, the worse it would have looked for him. I was sure he had taken a gamble. My response was, "You left Mr. Davies and he's alive and well. You return to the house within seconds, how could anyone else possibly have been involved?"

He replied, **"I never done John. We went round the green, we weren't going fast, it was more than a few seconds".**

I said, "What did you do when you saw him"?

He replied, **"I almost puked. I never killed him, I just cleared off.**

I again asked him if he went upstairs and he said that he hadn't.

When asked if he touched John he replied, **"Yes, I just touched his arm, I never killed him, people knew John was to go, people like George Bainbridge. John was shouting his mouth off; no way was I going to get done with John. I never hit him".**

I said, "You knew he would be there, asleep on the sofa!"

He replied, **"I didn't touch him, I never hit him with anything. I never splattered John".**

I said, "There are traces of blood over your clothing, your shirt and trousers.

He replied, **"I never hit John".**

I said, "You couldn't get blood on you in any other way".

He replied, **"I never killed him".**

When asked how long he had been in the house, Latham said, **"I felt 'pukey' and looked over the back of the sofa then left. He was gargling, rasping, that bloke was dead but there was air in the body".**

I said, "Why not call an ambulance or call the police?"

He said, **"I shit myself".**

I said, "Why?".

He replied, **"What happened to him, could happen to me. John's got a lot of money".**

I said, "What did you tell Danny?"

He replied, **"John's been done for. He said, who done it, you have, he said". There was a price on John. £3,000.**

DCI Bullock said, "That's rubbish and you know it, we are talking about a middle-aged man in Kidderminster who may be described as a petty thief or handler at most,"

He said, **"John told me, I told Phil and Danny".**

DCI Bullock – "Why do that?"

He replied, **"I wanted to find out if they knew anything".**

DCI Bullock – "How did John know?"

He replied, **"I don't know, he's crossed some people".**

DCI Bullock – "I find the whole story of this contract absolutely ludicrous. If you want to find out if Danny and Phil knew who set up this contract, all you've got to do is ask them, why say you've put the price on his head?"

He replied, **"Danny is the big 'I am' in this town. I expected him to come back at me and say, "no, you haven't, it's so and so."**

I said, "Are you trying to tell me that after finding John murdered, you calmly walk out to his daughter and say nothing and then drive through Kidderminster to your friend Danny, stopping en route for petrol it seems. You then tell Danny you've found John dead?"

He replied, **"I didn't kill him, I know I'm going to get life, I know that. I'd rather do life than walk out onto that street and get splattered. I can only confess that I found him dead."**

I said, "Well who do you say is responsible?"

He said, **"I'll get splattered if I say".**

I said, "The blood on your clothing could only have been caused at the time of the murder".

He replied, **"I can't account for it. I didn't kill John and don't know who did."**

I said, "Well, how do you explain the blood?"

He replied, **"I can't but I didn't splatter John."**

I said, "I want you to think carefully and go through it again."

He replied, **"I was going to go to Danny's anyway. I had no intention of going to the garage."**

I said, "Did you tell Carol that you'd forgot your fags?"

He replied, **"Yes, we went straight round the block and back. I said, "Hang around Carol", I walked in, John was there. I don't understand why I went back, there was something, something clicked. I don't know."**

I said, "Take it step by step."

He replied, **"The back door was wide open. I went in and walked into the living room. I saw John on the sofa with the dogs around his head. I grabbed John's arm; it was by his side. I just didn't know what to do. He was obviously as good as dead. He was lying on his side. I think he had his arm under his head like this"** (shows right hand under right side of head).

I said, "How long were you in the room?"

He replied, **"Seconds, I didn't know what the hell to do."**

I said, "Did you pick up anything in the room?"

He replied, **"No, I just went straight out, looked around the back to see if anybody was about, I jumped in the car and away."**

I said, "What did you tell Caroline?"

He replied, **"I said nothing to nobody until I saw Danny, I knew it wasn't him, 'cause he was there."**

I said, "Why not report it immediately, why tell all the lies?"

He replied, **"I didn't splatter him, that's what I'm fucking scared of, I know it looked bad for me."**

I said, "Did you go upstairs?"

He replied, **"No, definitely not, I might have looked in the hall."**

I said, "Did you go in the bathroom?"

He replied, **"No, I didn't go up the stairs."**

DCI Bullock said, "How could you calmly walk out and say nothing to John's daughter?" The telephone was there, you could have saved his life if you had called an ambulance?"

Latham made no reply.

DCI Bullock persisted – "Well?"

Latham replied**, "I don't know how I kept so calm, I told Danny it was done. He said I'd done it, I said No."**

DCI Bullock said, "Why did you go to the hospital?"

He replied, **"I was feeling bad 'cause of the sight I saw. I wanted something to put me right. I wanted to keep Carol away. I called on Phil, he wasn't there."**

DCI Bullock said, "Tell me what instrument did you use?"

He replied, **"I did not kill John"**

DCI Bullock said, "Well who did then?"

He replied, **"I don't know".**

DCI Bullock said, "You've just told us you know, now you say you don't?"

He replied, **"I don't know, I can't tell you."**

I said, "You went back intending to have some confrontation with him, didn't you?"

Latham said, **"Why did I go back, I don't know for sure?"**

I said, "Did you see anybody at the house or in the vicinity?"

He replied, **"I don't remember, I know when I went in, it had been done within a minute."**

I said, "Why on earth did you not notify the police or ambulance? Even if you left the house to do it, if what you say is true?"

He replied, **"I ran like fuck, that bloke was dead. I was frightened to death, I panicked, I just wanted to get the fuck out of there."**

I said, "Do you know how much money, if any, John had provided for Carol?"

He replied, **"Five thousand, twenty thousand, eighty thousand. He kept changing his mind."**

I said, "You and Carol intended to get married so you would clearly benefit financially from his death."

Latham said, **"Why didn't I rob him then? I could have had more money out of him alive than dead."**

I said, "What do you mean?"

He replied, **"I might have got some money from the bank job."**

I said, "Why did you not tell us these things in the first place?"

He replied, **"I knew what conclusions you would come to; I knew I was a convicted man. I was scared, I just wanted to get out of it."**

I said, "When you went to Danny's, I suspect you cleaned yourself down and wiped blood off your clothing."

He replied, **"Yes, I did with water and a flannel. There was some on my knee, on my jacket above my heart. I just gave my jacket a wipe over.**

I said, "Well how on earth can you explain having blood on your shoulder area?"

He replied, **"It must have come off the dogs. They were on John and I got them off. I shouted "get out of it. They jumped down but they always fuss round you."**

I said, "But how can you explain the blood on your jacket above your heart?" He made no reply and when I said, "Well," he replied, **"I can't explain it."**

I said, "There is no reasonable explanation is there? You killed Mr Davies."

He responded – **"No I did not. John told me he was to be done. I asked him who, he didn't say who, he talked in riddles."**

I said, "Who would want to do that, what has he done to deserve being killed?"

He replied, **"I told Danny, I told John that I would find out. I tried to find out who would be capable."**

I said, "Tell me again? What did you tell Danny when you went to his flat yesterday afternoon"?

Latham said, **"I told him John had been done. I did tell Danny I had done it."**

I said, "You told Danny that you had done it then?"

It would be, of course, now plainly obvious to Latham that McLaughlin had told us at least something near the truth. He would have been probably aware that we would now know that Latham had told McLaughlin that he had killed him. So how on earth could he escape the corner he was in?

His response was, **"Yes, I just wanted to see his reaction"**

DCI Bullock said, "There is no doubt in my mind that you went out on that afternoon to set up an alibi for yourself. You went to Danny's then you went to Phil's, the hospital and Sheila's. You have tried to explain away things you said to Danny and Phil, you know Danny would have to tell us you confessed to the murder and you also knew that he and Phil would have to tell us that you put a contract on Mr Davies. Also, when we asked you last night about blood stains, you said if there were any on your clothes, you wouldn't be able to explain it. Having thought about it, you realise that that was possible and that you had better come up with an excuse, that is why you told us you found the body."

He replied, **"I knew you wouldn't believe me."**

DCI Bullock said, "John was a small-time receiver, who is going to put £3,000 on his head, we're not talking about a London gangster."

Latham responded, **"I'm going to do 'Life' I know that but I know I didn't do it, I didn't splatter John."**

I said, "Are you saying you were there when it was done?"

He replied, **"No I'm not, something drew me back to the house, I don't know what, it wasn't only the cigarettes."**

I said, "Well what did draw you back, as you say?"

He replied, **"I don't know, I wish to God I knew"**

I said, "You say you were in the house five minutes?"

He replied, **"I don't think it was that long, Look, I know how it looks, I had blood on my clothes, I admit seeing John dead and the time lapse is so short and I was in the house at the time."**

I responded, "You were in the house at the time then?"

He replied, **"That was a slip of the tongue, I should say I was in the area at the time of the death."**

I said, "Tell me again about the price of Mr Davies's head?"

He replied, **"I told Danny and Phil."**

When I asked him when that was, he replied, **"Maybe two weeks ago."**

I said, "But why tell Phil? He didn't know John at that time."

He replied, **"He may have heard something."**

I said, "They would want to know where you would get £3,000 from"

He replied, **"I told them I would sell the antiques in the house, that's stupid I know"**

I said, "Why did you tell them you had put the price on his head?"

He replied, **"It was me and Carol going to South Africa, he was asking too many questions. The only way you can get money in South Africa is by being a soldier, they accepted that."**

I said, "Have you got a job lined up out there?"

He replied, **"I've been in touch with 'Executive 'Recruitment Consultants' and there is a mining company out there where I'll be able to get a job."**

I said, "you've told us that you went to Worcester to buy weapons to use on a bank robbery. You were obviously prepared to carry arms and no doubt shoot anyone who got in your way. You are prepared to kill and there's no doubt in my mind that you killed John Davies."

He replied, **"That's conjecture, I didn't kill the cunt!"**

I said, "A cunt, was he?"

He replied, **"Well, he got me in all this shit."**

I said, "You've changed your story to try and account for the bloodstains which you knew would be found on your clothing and you cannot satisfactorily explain it away. Clearly you killed John Davies."

He replied, **"Well, you're wrong there."**

Conference Time

At 1.45pm DCI Bullock and myself left the room. It was time for another short conference with Det. Chief Superintendent Cole and others. From the ensuing ending of the interview, we undoubtedly would discuss the wisdom of additionally arresting Latham on suspicion of committing the murder. He had already been arrested for conspiracy to rob and steal metal. We had also decided to arrest Carol on suspicion of murdering her father.

In addition, it will be remembered that when Latham was interviewed first, by Detective Sergeant Griffiths, on the actual day of the murder, Latham first introduced his friend, Danny McLaughlin into the equation as someone he and Carol had visited that afternoon. It would have been unknown by Latham that officers were immediately despatched to interview McLaughlin and indeed, they recorded a witness statement from him.

In that statement, he recorded that they arrived at between 2.15pm and 2.30pm. This was, of course, in compliance with what Latham had told him to say. As instructed, he told the police officers that the purpose of their visiting him was about playing in the darts match the following evening.

He also recorded that Doug went immediately to the bathroom and that he followed him there after about a minute.

At that time, he obviously did not inform the officers about the true reason for this visit. He had recorded in his statement exactly what Latham had told him to say and as far as he (and Latham) were concerned, everything would have been going well to confirm their alibi plan.

However, it was the above interview which opened the door to the investigation even wider. More than likely in the belief that McLaughlin had spilled the beans, Latham had now implicated McLaughlin in every aspect of the admissions he had made.

He was involved in the procurement of guns to do a bank robbery and he had also been propositioned to kill John Davies by shooting him at Martley or later, from a location near to John's house.

With the knowledge that McLaughlin was aware that Latham had killed John and had agreed to help with his alibi, he agreed to record a witness statement. It obviously became very clear that McLaughlin's statement was just a cover-up and so with haste, Detective Chief Inspectors Mayne and Smith re-visited McLaughlin. He agreed to accompany them to the police station for a further interview.

In a similar vein, Phillip Breakwell had also been interviewed in the early stages of the investigation, but this was not until the following day: the day in fact when we were now interviewing Latham and Carol Davies. This day, on 28th January, which was the day following the murder.

Suffice to say here that when he was first interviewed, under caution, he made a statement, also under caution, in which he provided many details of conversations between Latham, Carol Davies and Danny McLaughlin about the obtaining of weapons, although he was unsure for what reason they were required.

He was later drawn into the idea being made about him being a getaway driver when John was to be shot. He stated that he believed that all this was 'Big Talk' and that he would never get involved in the killing of anyone. Indeed, he eventually contrived an injury to his knee which ensured that he would not be involved. He was duly bailed from the police station, pending further enquiries being made.

And so, it was following our management meeting that at 2pm DCI Bullock and myself continued our interview of Latham, albeit for a short period.

I said, "I told you earlier that you were under arrest for conspiracy to rob, you can now take it that you are arrested for suspicion of murder.

He replied, **"I shan't do any time'"**

I said, "You mean about your cancer?"

He said, **"No, I'll top myself."**

We finished our interview about five minutes later and Latham was returned to the cells at 2.05pm

None of us had managed to get sleep or visit our homes during this lengthy period, but so far as my main hobby of eating was then concerned, whilst 'Fine Dining' cannot be expected, police canteens have always been able to serve up wholesome food with chips and so my stomach was always content.

So, in addition to the main briefings of all those officers seconded to the Incident Room, us senior investigators would be using these dining times to have a good chat about progress and things to be done. On this occasion, after our meal, we moved from the canteen into the DCI's office to discuss which actions should be prioritised and who would pursue them.

By this time, Latham had been appointed a Mr. White, a solicitor from somewhere in the West Midlands to represent him. DCI Bullock and myself made him fully aware of where we were at that time and off we went to the Indian Restaurant at Comberton Hill for our evening meal. Again, these breaks and 'down time' were used to discuss our tactics and generally where we were with the investigation.

Having returned to the station, we found Mr. White in the Police Club and held a discussion with DCIs Mayne and Smith regarding their interview with Philip Breakwell and how deep he was involved in the conspiracy at that particular time.

14. – Carol Davies - 3rd Interview

We were now well past our second set of 24 hours duty since the commission of the murder and without sleep. The re-interviewing of the conspirators, McLaughlin and Breakwell, was to help enormously. Their versions could, of course, be compared with that of the two main suspects, Latham and Carol Davies, but they were making absolutely no admissions.

By changing his story and adding to it to suit himself, Latham had by now virtually cooked his goose and it was obvious that Carol was doing all she could to protect him. I must say at this juncture that my experience of interviewing her had already drawn me to the conclusion that she was the 'hardest' woman I had interviewed in my experience thus far. Obviously, we were all more experienced in interviewing men but when we interviewed women with something to hide, it was a normal occurrence for them to break down in tears and proverbially 'put their hands up'. – NOT SO for Miss Caroline Davies.

Even if she did hate her father, one cannot imagine that she would have anything to do with conspiring to kill him. After all, he doted on her and one would expect at least a tear to fall at the horrible way she helped dispose of him. Not one teardrop had fallen. Not to compare the analogy of what she suffered on the prior day, getting any useful information from her was like 'pulling teeth' except that these teeth never even became loose. There was little she would divulge, unless it was in the knowledge that we already knew the answers.

However, there being no direct evidence to charge her prior to us interviewing Latham, she had been released. Unbeknown to DCI Bullock and myself, she had gone or been taken to her neighbour's house at number 11 Clifton Road.

It was now, however, necessary to re-interview her and at 8.30pm on that same evening, Wednesday 28th January, Detective Sergeant Griffiths and WDC Jones arrested her there on suspicion of murdering her father. She was placed in custody at the Police Station.

So, it wasn't until later that evening, at 9.07pm on the day after the murder, 28th January 1981, that DCI Bullock and myself interviewed her again with Det. Inspector Herbert writing the notes. Woman Det. Constable Jones was with us, but took no part in the interview.

It might be easier to understand if I provide here a summary of what she told us in answer to our questions. The advantage is that I can omit much of the information adduced from her in previous interviews and concentrate on her contribution based on the questions which were formed following the interviews of the others involved. Being now under arrest, she was interviewed after being cautioned.

We had learned that the final idea on how John was to be killed was by shooting him and indeed it was to take place on the Sunday prior to when he was actually killed. The day before, they had all visited the location behind the house to set up an escape route after the killing and Carol had warned whoever was required to escape about the dangers of falling over the barbed wire in the dark. This was put to Carol and she avoided the question by saying "I don't know what you're talking about, I didn't kill him, are you suggesting I killed my dad?"

She was continually pressed as to the reason why she had told so many lies, especially as we were investigating the death of her father. She continually avoided answering questions directly, by saying that she didn't kill him. She finally admitted that "We thought about it, yes."

When asked about who it was that thought about planning to kill her dad, she replied, "It was me, he kept nagging me and picking faults, we needed a couple of thousand and then we thought we could go."

She said this was Doug and her and that her dad had told her that he would be leaving her some money in his will.

This was obviously the time when she would have realised that we knew from McLaughlin and Breakwell exactly what the plans had been prior to his death. It seemed to us that she was now having to admit to some sort of conspiracy to kill her dad but that she had no hand in the actual killing.

DCI Bullock asked her how it was that they intended to kill him, she replied "Shoot him, we made enquiries with George we tried to get guns. The idea was to shoot him by the back door or in Stourbridge Road."

She said that the plans were made during the previous three weeks.

When pressed more to describe the method and tell us who would carry out the shooting, she said that they thought it would be best to shoot him through the windscreen as he drove along the Stourbridge Road, on his way to sell some scrap. Either Doug or Danny would do the shooting; Danny had also hated her dad, through past associations with him when they worked together.

I then raised the subject of paying Danny money for the assassination and she agreed that she offered Danny one thousand pounds. He wanted £1,000 per shot and it would take three shots. However, she said that Danny offered to do the shooting for free, so long as he was able to join her and Doug on their emigration to South Africa.

Danny had falsely told them that he had recently been arrested for stabbing someone and was on bail. This story turned out to be completely fictitious. In fact, he had been arrested for the non-payment of maintenance arrears for his wife and child. This was in the earlier days, when Latham and he were trying to win the bragging rights connected with their escapades and only goes to indicate what braggarts and Walter Mitty characters they were.

When asked who else was to be involved, she said that Phil Breakwell was going to drive a getaway car and that Danny would be in the Bridge pub to provide him with an alibi. She explained that this planning had occurred during the week prior to when Danny had been arrested for the stabbing (fictitious). She said, **"I got fed up with dad picking on me all the time about the housework and getting up earlier and not taking mum to work."**

She agreed that it was the money in the back of her mind and that they wanted to get away from it all. However, she persisted with saying that it wasn't her who killed him. Her dad had told her that he had left two thirds of the money in his bank accounts to her and that her mum would have the house and insurance pay out.

She thought that her share would be about two to four thousand pounds.

Their idea, she said, was to possibly go to Germany first and then on to South Africa. They had already sent away for visas and passports and were hoping to travel in a van and live in it for a while. She said that she thought that the applications were made in late November and that this was with the agreement of her dad.

So, returning to the plan to kill her dad, she said that all agreed that shooting him was the best way. She said, **"Danny said it was the best way. We talked about it in the Bridge before Phil came back. Danny was going to do it. I only wanted one shot, one bullet in the chest, that's all it needed. Me and Doug were going to provide the alibi."**

I questioned the fact about Danny wanting to make it three shots and a thousand pounds for each one. She reiterated that it only would take one shot and that he was only going to get one thousand pounds, but when the stabbing charge came along, he changed his mind and wanted to go along with them to South Africa instead.

She then explained about getting the guns and that her dad had planned the bank job so Danny approached the George in Sion Hill, later proved to be George Bettis. Plans were made to meet another George from Wrexham. This was confusing at first, because he was indeed from Wrexham though he had been temporarily staying at an address at Northfield Street in the Arboretum area of Worcester. It will be recalled that this other George (Bainbridge) was said to be an ex-SAS man who told Doug that he could kill him.

So, the subject then changed to Phil Breakwell's involvement and I asked her when he had first become involved. She explained that when they had all gone to Worcester to meet George, Phil went along with Danny and Doug and was with them when they were at George Bettis's home at Sion Hill, when the other George had failed to turn up. Danny had said that he wanted someone with him when the shooting was to happen and Phil was mentioned but that she couldn't remember who it was that asked Phil.

When asked about the cost of the guns, she told us that it would be £100. Fifty pounds from Doug and fifty pounds from her dad.

It must, of course, be remembered that so far as John was concerned, the guns were for a robbery that he was planning. So far as the four conspirators were concerned, they only wanted one gun to kill Carol's dad.

This is a conundrum which is so bizarre that at some time, and I think now is as good as any, speculation by the local investigators was stretched to a scenario which, I stress, cannot be proved but may not be too far from the truth.

I have already mentioned that the deceased, John Davies, may have been a small-time informant to the local police. I was not part of the local CID and I do not know whether that is correct or not but all I can say is that it had been mentioned: by whom I genuinely do not know.

Police enquiries made following his death give rise to suspicion that because of his displeasure about his daughter's associates, he hatched a plan to involve Latham and McLaughlin in a conspiracy to commit the armed robbery for which they would have to obtain firearms. There was no doubt that, at some suitable stage, he would have informed on both of them thus offering them up to the police as sacrificial lambs and, in his estimation, removing them from the company of, and influence upon his daughter, for some considerable time.

The incongruous situation therefore had developed whereby Latham and McLaughlin were making attempts to secure firearms to pursue their plan to dispose of Mr Davies, whilst he was encouraging them to obtain weapons to rob a bank. For this reason, the two conspiracies became interwoven.

Danny McLaughlin and John had argued over obtaining the money to get the guns and John had refused saying that Danny had told him that they would be free for inspection and approval first.

One can imagine that if the above assumption was correct, then John would not have wanted to have been brought into the frame as an 'agent provocateur' by putting up funds to obtain weapons. If he had been setting the boys up to get caught, then by putting up the money, he would have put himself into the same level as the others in robbing the bank. Who would have believed him, if he had somehow been drawn into being arrested during the earlier than anticipated plan?

The law simply states that anyone who aids, abets, counsels or procures the commission of a criminal offence can be arrested and charged as one of the principals.

I emphasise whilst that may have been true, so far as I'm concerned, I cannot vouch one iota that that was the case. So far as I'm aware, John's plan to rob the bank at Barbourne, Worcester, was a genuine plan but which version is correct, I cannot say.

Anyway, back to our interview with Carol. She said that Danny wanted to look at the house although he had been there before, but he was not available and so Phil went.

It was Phil who was going to steal a car from the hospital car park and drive Danny who would be doing the shooting. She said, **"We took him round the back and showed him the garages. I told him to watch the barbed wire. Danny wanted to kill him by the back door. Phil wanted to go the front way. Phil also had a look at the best road out."**

It was then that I asked her where she went on the previous Saturday night. She said that she went to the Bridge Inn but Phil **wasn't there because he had hurt "his leg or something"**

This statement, confirms of course what Breakwell himself said after his arrest, in that during the short time that he had got himself involved with these characters, he had assumed that their so-called plans were just pub 'Big Talk'. It would have been this activity that Carol had been describing which caused him to feign his injury and which would thus prevent him from driving the getaway car.

I then changed the subject to the activities of the two when they had returned to the house to collect something that Doug had left behind. I said, "We now know that when Doug got back in the car after collecting his cigarettes, your father was dead – murdered."

She replied, **"What? You're mad, I don't believe it, Doug wouldn't do it'"**

I told her that he may have had blood on his hands and clothing because there were traces on the steering wheel. She said that she hadn't seen any and when told that he had washed it off his clothes at Danny's, she said that she didn't believe it.

I then said to her, "You have told us that you, Doug, Danny and Phil planned to kill your father. Are you telling us that someone else beat you to it?"

She made the same reply as she had done all along, in that when backed into a corner, she simply would say, **"I didn't kill him."**

When told that Doug's clothes were spattered with blood consistent with having committed the murder, she said, **"he wouldn't do it like that, not like that."**

I then informed her that Doug had told us that he wiped the blood off in Danny's bathroom. "Surely you must have seen it, or at least he must have said something to you? He'd just left your father lying on the sofa with his head caved in."

She replied, **"He seemed perfectly normal to me."** It was also put to her that he must have been in the house longer than 30 seconds and she responded by saying that it didn't seem long.

She also said that it was Doug's idea to go to Danny's and that they had not gone to Phil's, but she couldn't remember if they tried to find him.

DCI Bullock asked her whose idea it was to go to the hospital and she said that it was her idea, but neither her or Doug would have killed her dad like that. She explained that Doug and Danny were only in Danny's bathroom for two minutes and that they just drank coffee.

DCI Bullock put it to her that Doug had told us that there was blood on his shoulder, but she denied seeing it. He also told her that the original plan was that they would kill her dad, so if he did it, he would have told her. She responded that **"he wouldn't have done it like that, he wouldn't have had the nerve."**

Carol was plainly telling us that although they planned to kill her father, Doug wouldn't have done it that way. The inference being that it would be more straightforward and less messy to have shot him. But of course, they had no weapons with which to shoot him.

She then agreed that she hated her father but when asked if it was her plan that he be killed on that day, which then, would be described as 'yesterday', she said, **"No, I had no idea, I wouldn't do it like that."**

In response to me telling her that they had no guns, so they needed to change plans, she again withdrew to the stock answer, **"I didn't kill him."**

I asked her if Danny or Phil could have done it and she said that they couldn't, because Danny was at the flat decorating and neither he nor Phil had cars.

I then told Carol that Doug had told us that when he got to Danny's, he told him that he had killed her dad. She again denied that Doug would have done it that way.

So, I asked her if I had told her that her dad had been shot by him, would she have believed that? She said that she would, as that was the way they had planned to kill him.

When I asked her what the difference was, she said that it was a lot different leaving him in that way so that her mother would find him in that condition.

It must be said that all this explanation about it not being the plan to bludgeon John to death, is, on the face of it, quite feasible. Could it be that it was a sudden impulse to return and find an iron bar anywhere in the garden, knowing that John was asleep on the settee, in the house alone. Could it have been a spontaneous moment and a strong desire to have him killed that led to the decision to kill John there and then, or was it even planned to return to the house to kill him? Whichever way, there was no doubt in our minds that it was Latham who killed him, even without a plan or with Carol's prior knowledge.

It was due to what Carol said at Danny's when she asked him on his return from the bathroom whether he had told him that, whatever the plan or no plan, Carol was now protecting him. The other thing to bear in mind is when was it that the alibi commenced – visiting the dentist, visiting the jeweller's shop, visiting Danny's and the hospital or when? If it was in the morning at any time, then that would confirm that the plan was indeed to kill him that day, but we remain unsure.

The fact that he needed to escape the house quickly and to tidy himself up may well have been the motivation for visiting Danny's flat and the hospital because there is evidence at both locations that he was cleaning blood off himself and his clothes.

So far as the hospital was concerned, I had created an 'action' for the toilets there to be thoroughly searched, as there could well be the remnants of evidence of cleaning himself up there too.

Lo and behold, it was Detective Constable Willetts who was assigned the action and who found a freshly blood-soaked handkerchief tucked behind a cistern in one of the gents' water closets. It was hidden and could not be seen unless the searcher's head was right against the wall.

The blood was the same group as that of John Davies's but of course, this was 1981, some five years before DNA analysis was used for the first time in Leicestershire to convict a murderer (Colin Pitchfork) of killing two young girls.

Carol persisted in the idea that Doug would not have done it that way and even if it hadn't been Doug who was responsible, he would surely have told her that her father had been murdered?

It was then that she demonstrated her hardness and lack of remorse.

She had obviously lied when telling us that they never went to the canal. They were together and would have been aware that Doug had thrown something heavy into the canal. We would have become aware of that later, but here she was, trying to protect him. She said, **"No, if he did, I wouldn't have left him for mum to find. He would have told me. You're lying."**

So, it was plain to see that she knew very well what Latham had done and that her mother was now left in that terrible position of having to find her husband who'd been killed in such a barbaric way and in such a mess.

In answering how long it was between the time of leaving the house and returning there, Carol exclaimed that it was only seconds, they just drove around the green. She drove a rough plan as to their route and the distance was negligible.

I put it to her that it was ridiculous to suggest that in that short space of time, someone else had entered the house and killed her father. It was then that she rested on the excuse of feeling dopey due to her mass extraction of teeth earlier that morning.

She continued that when she was sitting in the car waiting for Doug, she wasn't particularly aware of seeing people other than a lady with a little child, but because she was walking away from her, she didn't know who it was.

She assured us that she had been telling the truth and that there was nothing else she wanted to say and the interview terminated at 10.20pm. (28th Jan.) She was returned to the cells whilst DCI Bullock, DI Herbert and I got together to record our notebooks from DI Herbert's jottings. We had finished at 12.10am that night but DCI Bullock was called away at 11.15pm.

This was the first opportunity for us to go to bed. I recall that during the latter period of the inquiry, it was normal at the conclusion of the day's business to grab a pint or two at the Kidderminster Police Club but I think we had to sacrifice that, as I recall the Assistant Chief Constable, Alan Vickers, almost directing us to go home.

After all, the main suspects were now in custody and the last time we had gone to bed was during the late evening of 26th January, now roughly two days ago. Perhaps in our slumbers, we could dream that the West Midlands Police Underwater search unit would be able to find the murder weapon in the canal during the next day, Thursday 29th January.

15. - Gone Fishing

What none of us had realised at that time, was that about 2.15pm on the day of the murder, at roughly the time when the murder was committed, a Mr. Millward had settled down at the canal running through Kidderminster after he had finished his day's work. He commenced to fish about fifteen to twenty yards away from Caldwell Hills Bridge on the new Road side of the canal. This bridge was located not far from where he lived between Park Lane and New Road, Kidderminster, next to the Brinton's Carpet factory car park.

At about 2.45pm to 3pm, he saw a silver-grey Vauxhall Viva car stop right in the middle of the bridge. There were two people in the front seats of the car. Although he did not see the driver, he saw that there was a young lady in the passenger seat. The vehicle remained stationary for about five minutes. The next thing that he heard was a splash and the vehicle drove off at speed.

As the vehicle drove off behind him, he turned around to see the registration number of it. He thought it was EOK 378 H but he was more certain of the numbers and the suffix letter 'H' than the first three letters. The registration number of Carol's vehicle was in fact UOK 378 H. Mr. Millward had remembered the number correctly, all except for the very first letter which was a letter 'U' and not a letter 'E' as he had recalled.

He had assumed that maybe some unwanted puppies or whatever, had been thrown into the canal. Following a police appeal for sightings of Carol's Vauxhall car that day, it was during the evening of the following day, Wednesday 28th January whilst reading the police appeal in the local newspaper, and at about the same time as we had been last interviewing Carol Davies, that he saw the significance of what he had observed by the canal.

He notified Kidderminster Police Station.

Of course, this was such an important breakthrough, or at least it showed all the signs of being such, that at 11.50pm on that night, when DI Peter Herbert and I were making up our pocket notebooks, DCI Bullock had earlier left us to be shown by Mr. Millward, exactly where he was fishing and the relevant locations of what he had witnessed. He did the same at 1.40pm on the following day, when he showed the members of the West Midlands Police Underwater Search Unit the same.

It was because Ian Bullock had been interrupted whilst Peter Herbert and I were making up our pocket books, that Ian later signed my pocket book agreeing that what we had recorded was correct. This was necessary and saved him copying the same into his own notebook.

Although this witness was unable to see the driver at all, he described the passenger, a young woman with dark coloured shoulder length hair and approximately 20 to 30 years of age.

By the time I had got home that night and booked off duty, it was 1.15am Not having slept too well, I was back at Kidderminster Police Station at 9.10am. I don't think I was made aware of the find until the following day, when I arrived at the police station for what was to become an early morning briefing of what had been achieved during the past two days and what still needed to be done. Of course, the main item on the agenda was the finding of the witness, Mr Millward.

In addition, of course, the many officers carrying out routine enquiries generated by 'actions' were also there so that they could contribute their activities since their last briefing. Whilst there was no doubt about the fact that both Latham and Carol Davies were heavily involved in John's death, the details that Mr Millward was able to bring to the table, were able to be shared among the whole team. This brought a huge uplift to the morale of everyone who had been working many hours on the actions they had been allotted.

The sighting of Carol's vehicle on the canal bridge, which was not on the route they had described, was exciting enough - but would we be able to recover what had been thrown into the canal?

Was this going to be our chance to recover the murder weapon?

So, apart from poor DCI Ian Bullock who was not allowed to have as long a sleep as myself, it was not just some of us interviewers who had the opportunity to sleep, but also Latham and Carol in police custody. Plans were being made for a special sitting of the Kidderminster Magistrates Court for the following day, Friday 30th January.

Before that, however, there was further business to be had with them both, including DCI Bullock's late night with Mr Millward showing him and other officers the location where he had seen the Vauxhall and its two occupants on the canal bridge.

We had a choice to refrain from interviewing our suspects about Mr. Millward's evidence until the underwater search team had done their job but the momentum of the day was with us. In any event, what if they were unable to find what it was that had been thrown into the canal? Apart from one letter, the registration number of their vehicle and the general description of it had been 'clocked' at the canal, which was completely off the route which they had individually described.

There was no holding us back. Today, Thursday 29th January 1981, was going to be our day. So far, receiving admissions from both of them had only been achieved when they knew that what they told us could be proved or when they thought that by admitting what they had done, was necessary in the uncertainty of what others, McLaughlin and Breakwell in particular, might well have told us.

1. Had someone seen them return to the house so soon after leaving it?

2. Would forensics be able to find blood on Latham's clothes?

3. Had McLaughlin told the police of the conversation he had with Latham in the bathroom?

4. Would Breakwell hold his nerve? Although he knew little, he had been taken over the escape route and had agreed to be the escape car driver after John had been shot. What had he told the police?

5. Would the real relationships between Carol, her dad and Latham be discovered or would this front of a happy household, with Latham being regarded as John's son, be maintained?

All these things and more had been going through their heads and by admitting what they had, they were just pre-empting what might obviously be discovered. These were the only things admitted.

But now, neither of them had pre-empted the fact that a fisherman would be fishing close to that canal bridge and was astute enough to suspect that the occupants of their car were up to no good, possibly disposing of a sack full of unwanted puppies, or whatever. AND he had almost exactly recalled the correct registration number of their car. There was certainly no holding us back.

16. - Carol Davies – 4th Interview

So, it was approximately four hours off two full days since John Davies had met his untimely death on Tuesday 27th January, when his beloved daughter was again brought from the cells to attend at the DCI's office at Kidderminster Police Station.

Thanks to his late-night visit to the canal side, DCI Ian Bullock had not had as much sleep as the rest of us. However, he had been only too pleased to be taken to the spot on the canal by Mr. Millward for a run through what he had seen and heard. For that reason, it was he who was also very pleased to kick off the interview with Carol. DCI Herbert was again to record the notes and WDC Jones was also present.

DCI Bullock asked her how she felt that morning and she managed to squeeze out a modicum of compassion by saying that she was alright but that it was her mother who she felt sorry about. Yes, this was the mother who we had discovered would also be murdered later, if all of their plans had gone their way.

DCI Bullock cautioned her again and asked her several questions about the vehicle they were in and which route they took when they drove to see Danny at his girlfriend's maisonette.

She was unable to recite the exact registration number but said that it was a Vauxhall Viva and the suffix letter was an 'H'. She said that she had already told us that Doug was driving, she was in the passenger seat and that they had travelled along Walter Nash Road, Stourport Road, Ring Road and into The Horsefair. Importantly, there was no mention of the Caldwell Hills canal bridge.

She agreed that she was absolutely sure that that was the route they took to arrive at Danny's.

DCI Bullock said, "Last night I spoke to a man who had been standing near to the canal bridge next to Brinton's car park at about a quarter to three yesterday. He saw your car on the bridge and he saw something being thrown from the car into the canal.

She replied, **"We didn't go by the canal."**

DCI Bullock said, "He has described you and eventually, we shall discover what it was you threw into the canal."

She again replied, **"We didn't go down by the canal."**

DCI Bullock said, "Somebody saw you and can describe you and your vehicle. He saw details of your car in the paper and came up to the Police Station to tell us what he had seen. Your father has been murdered yet you sit there telling lie after lie."

She made no reply and then when DCI Bullock said, "Well?" She said, **"We went to the canal. Yes, yes, yes. Now you know."**

When asked what was thrown in, she said, **"I don't know, I was half asleep, it was Doug"**

When DCI Bullock asked her where he got it from, she said, **"Between the driver's door and the seat."**

DCI Bullock said, "What was it?" She replied, **"I don't know. His underpants and something big and long. I was half asleep."**

I said, **"Let me tell you something else we know, when you went to Danny's, you said to Doug in front of Danny, "Have you told him?" I believe you were referring to the fact that you had killed your father."**

She replied, **"I didn't say that, I said, "Has he asked you? I meant playing darts. It was either that or I said to Doug, "Have you asked him?" I was trying to find out if Danny knew he was playing darts the next day."**

I said, "This object that he threw into the canal; where did it come from?"

She replied, **"Doug brought it into the car when he fetched the fags."**

I said, "What did you see?"

She replied, **"I saw his underpants, some blue towelling ones."**

When asked what else she said, **"It looked like a big piece of rotten wood."**

I asked her if the underpants were wrapped around it between his hand and the object and she replied, **"Yes, they looked wet, I think they were out of the washing. I think they were the ones I put to soak with the socks and hankies."**

I said, "how long was the object?"

She replied, **"About a foot."**

I said, "Did he take anything out of the car into the house?"

She replied, **"No."**

I then asked her if she recognised the object and she said, **"No. It could have been a bit of scrap, a bar I suppose."**

I said, "Just now you said the item he carried out looked like a rotten piece of wood, then you say, it could have been a bar. This is very important, think carefully, what exactly was it?"

She said, **"It could have been one of those spanner things dad had by the back door, I don't know."**

I said, "You obviously asked him what he was doing with the pants and the bar?"

She replied, **"Yea, I said, "What you got them for?" He just said "Nothing".**

Carol agreed that he had thrown the pants and the bar into the canal but when asked what she said to him about it, she said, **"I didn't bother that much, I didn't say anything."**

I said, "I find that very difficult to accept. You tell us that you saw Doug leave the house with a bar wrapped in a pair of his underpants and you go to the canal and he drops them in. How do you expect anyone with common sense to believe you don't question him about it?"

She replied, **"I told you, I was half asleep."**

I said, "You must have gone to the garage and paid for petrol seconds before. You got out of the car to do that so you were well awake then, weren't you?"

She made no reply and I said, "The fact that you did not tell us this about the bar and pants being thrown into the canal can only mean that you're protecting Doug and yourself."

She said, **"I forgot to tell you. I didn't do it, if you think I did, you prove it."**

I said, "Last night, you sat there and told me that you had been truthful and had no more information. How can anyone believe you're not involved?"

She replied, **"I told you I forgot about the canal."**

DCI Bullock quickly responded, "But when questioned about it in detail, you denied it."

She replied, **"Look, I forgot. I didn't kill him."**

As mentioned before, whenever she had backed herself into a corner, she frequently ducked a proper answer by just saying, "I didn't kill him".

I said, "Danny has been truthful I believe, he has even told us about a burglary at Martley that he did with Latham and you. Is that correct?"

She replied, **"Yes, I drove the car, it was a cottage near the one dad owns, we flogged the stuff in Worcester."**

When asked more about the property taken and where it was sold, she described a couple of brass candlesticks, wooden elephants and a couple of clocks. She said that it was all sold in different places in Worcester, one was by the dual carriageway, by the police station.

DCI Bullock said, "Did you really go back to the house, or is that a lie?

She replied, **"Yes, he was alright when we left a few seconds before."**

DCI Bullock said, "How long was Doug in the house?"

She replied, **"It didn't seem long I'm sure, half a minute about."**

DCI Bullock said, "I suspect you went in the house."

She replied, **"I didn't, I tell you, I didn't"**

DCI Bullock said, "The truth is slowly unfolding and it is only when putting specific matters to you in detail, do you appear to tell the truth. Tell us what really did happen."

She replied, **"I told you, I sat in the car and as far as I know, he went in to get the fags."**

DCI Bullock said, "You have told us lies right from the start. You didn't mention going back for the cigarettes until it was put to you. You didn't mention Doug feeling sick until it was put to you. You were telling lies to protect him even before we viewed him as a suspect, so it seems you must have known he was involved."

She replied, **"I didn't know".**

I said, "Tell us of any conversation you had with him."

She simply replied, **"If he did it, he should pay for it."**

I said, "Look, you saw Doug carry a bar from the house wrapped in a pair of underpants and he then threw them in the canal. How can you say you didn't ask him all about it?"

She replied, **"I didn't think it was important. I also saw him throw something else away, it looked like white material, in the waste chute by Danny's. There, I've told you everything I know."**

I asked her when was it that she saw Doug throw this away in the waste chute and she replied, **"When we got to Danny's flat before we got to the door."** She explained that it was **"soft, something you could squeeze into your hand, it was sticking out through his fingers."**

Following this disclosure, a search was made of the chute and bin at Danny's flat as quickly as possible, but nothing of any significance was found.

I said, "Why lie to us all of the time?"

She replied, **"I don't know. I thought he may have done it I suppose, but I couldn't believe he could have done it like that."**

I said, "I think you took the opportunity to kill your father, you had planned to do it for some time, you knew he would be asleep on the sofa alone, an ideal chance."

She replied, **"I wouldn't bash him on the head, I wouldn't let mum go in and find him if I knew he was dead like that."**

The time was now 11.20am on Thursday 29th January and DCI Bullock and I left the room leaving Detective Inspector Herbert and WDC Jones with Carol with the intention of her being asked to record a written statement of what she had told us. However, before that procedure commenced, Detective Inspector Herbert said to her, "If we accept that Doug didn't tell you that he had killed your father, when you both got home and you were told by the police and your mother what had happened, you must have thought about the bar being thrown in the canal and realised that Doug had killed him. You were together in the neighbour's house, surely you said something to him?"

She replied, **"I thought it might have been him. I asked him if he had done it. He said that he hadn't but told me to be careful what I was saying to the police as they would try to blame us."**

D.I. Herbert continued to ask her about Doug's reactions and her involvement but she intimated to him that she would be going down for this, so why should she lie any more.

DI Herbert said to her, "Danny has told us that Doug told him that he had murdered your father."

She replied, **"I remember now, Danny and Doug giggling together. I wondered what it was all about, I thought it might be about my teeth."**

D.I. Herbert said, "I find it quite incredible that minutes after leaving your father lying dead with his head smashed in, Latham is giggling with a friend in his flat and yet you protect him by lying to us."

She replied, **"He's not worth protecting."**

After indicating that she was telling the truth and there was nothing else she could say, DI Herbert asked her if she would like to make a statement about what she had said. She indicated that she would and that she would prefer WDC Jones to write it, as opposed to writing it herself.

Just to remind readers that, as opposed to a witness statement, which can be completely structured by the police officer recording it, this will be a defendant statement, made under caution.

Carol had signed a caption to the statement before starting it which said-

> **"I Caroline Davies wish to make a statement. I want someone to write down what I say. I have been told that I need not say anything unless I wish to do so and that whatever I say may be given in evidence."**

Whilst there would be no harm in the officers guiding the maker as to the subject matter designed to be covered, the content of her statement will be what she says and how she describes it herself.

Furthermore, a further caption would be signed by the maker at the conclusion of the statement. That caption states: -

> **"I have read the above statement and I have been told that I can correct, alter or add anything I wish. This statement is true, I have made it of my own free will."**

In addition to Carol signing that caption, she also signed at the foot of every page and there were 30 pages in total. The statement was recorded between 12.10pm and 10.20pm. That is ten hours and ten minutes.

The final page of the statement carries details of who was present during its making and of all refreshment and other breaks. It recorded who was present other than DI Herbert and WDC Jones, who actually wrote the statement. Their signatures and the signatures of those others present are recorded. In this case, breaks were taken at 2.05pm and 2.15pm and at 3.17pm and 4.12pm.

In addition to the two officers, the following were present: -

Mrs Rollason of Weston's Solicitors, between 4.12pm and 6.50pm.

Mr. R. Jones of the same company of solicitors, between 5.40pm and 10.20pm. Additional breaks were taken between 7.25pm and 7.34pm. and between 8.45pm and 8.53pm for consultation with Mr Jones.

Meals were supplied at 12.45pm and 5.30pm.

Much of what Carol included in her statement was adduced from the questions posed to her by the interviews already summarised. The statement commenced by her explaining that she had told lots of lies but now wished to tell the truth. She commenced by giving a thorough background to what had happened that day, including how she and Douglas Latham first got together and how their plans to emigrate evolved.

She touched on the friction that grew about her doing nothing much but lying in bed and going to the pub with Latham. Tension grew between herself and her dad. Because of his nagging, at times she grew to hate him, although Doug and her dad seemed to get on well together.

From this place onward, when it becomes necessary to make a comment on what Carol has included in her statement, I will turn the text into italics, as it might be misleading if the comment is not differentiated from the facts she included in her statement.

She stated that a few weeks back "before Danny got done for stabbing," (*He was never arrested for stabbing* though *he was arrested in connections with the non-payment of maintenance for his wife and child*) Danny and Doug had been talking together in the Bridge Inn whilst she was playing on a 'Space Invader' machine. Danny approached her and said, "It's a shame we can't bump your dad off, he must be worth a bit". She laughed this off but later, on the way home, Doug suggested that it wasn't a bad idea, because they could get some money and go abroad. With what she knew of her dad's finances and his will, she reckoned she would get about £4,000. She grew to like the idea, so long as there were no 'come backs'.

At a later meeting of the three in the Bridge Inn, Danny asked her if she could get her mum and dad out of the house somewhere quiet and she snapped back that it was only her dad to be killed. Doug later asked her what she felt about shooting her dad as Danny could get a gun. She responded that she didn't mind that, as it would be done quickly with no pain.

Danny had disappeared for a few days. When he was next in the pub, he explained that he had been arrested for stabbing someone at a party and his case had been adjourned for a month. He wanted to escape the court appearance and said that he would shoot her dad for £1,000, but it was normal to be paid £1,000 per shot. This was when she said that it would only take one shot.

It was later that Phillip Breakwell, the soldier on leave from the Army in Germany, came on the scene as he was included in the conversations about shooting her dad. Danny had apparently stated that he would like someone with him when he shot John and that maybe they could encourage Phil as he was a soldier. They would befriend him before making the suggestion. Eventually this was put to Phil and he wanted £700 to buy himself out of the Army. *(For all intents and purposes, the conspiracy to kill her father was complete).*

She explained that Danny's case had later been adjourned again and that he was suggesting that as he was bound to 'go down' he would rather join them in their quest to emigrate than be paid the £1,000.

She then described her dad sitting on her bed one morning after taking her mum to work just after he had feared losing his job for being drunk at work. He said that he suspected he might lose his job and so he was going to disappear for a while to do a bank job to get enough money to retire on.

However, he explained that he wanted four others on the job and some automatic guns and ammunition. As he left her, he said that he didn't mind if she told Doug.

(It would appear here that, by dropping this information to Carol, she was bound to bring Doug and McLaughlin into being involved. This would suit John if he had planned to inform on them, but as emphasised earlier, that was just conjecture.)

She wasted no time and it wasn't long before the three of them were discussing it. She said that Doug was all for it because they would get their money to emigrate without having to kill her dad.

They had tipped off Danny about this plan. Sure enough, he was later enrolled into the conspiracy to rob at a meeting John had with Danny in the Bridge pub. John later told Doug and Carol that Danny had told him that he could get guns from an ex-SAS man and that no money would be required to see them on approval. He would want £100 however, if they were to be used.

The ex-SAS man turned out to be George Bettis from Sion Hill, Kidderminster *(who had never been in the SAS).* He told Danny that he needed to arrange the guns through another George (Bainbridge) also an ex-SAS man who he could arrange to meet during the next day at Worcester. *(George Bainbridge was, in fact, from Wrexham but had been placed in temporary accommodation by the Probation department having been acquitted at Worcester Crown Court on a charge of Arson.)*

It is doubtful whether he could spell SAS, let alone be in the Army at all. So, this is where it's necessary to deviate from Carol's statement to explain what a comedy of errors had occurred when   Doug and Phil, led by Danny, were sent on a wild goose-chase to Worcester to meet this George Bainbridge.

George Bettis had known George Bainbridge and, some years previously, had enrolled him as something of a 'bouncer type' character to assist with putting the 'frighteners' on a man who was then having an association with his estranged wife. His wife had returned to the matrimonial home and this venture never actually took place.

Bettis had given Danny the last address he had for Bainbridge, unaware that he had since moved. Danny, Doug and Phil had called at the address to learn that Bainbridge no longer lived there but they were given the idea that he frequented the Miramar Café, in Worcester. It was there that they hung around all day and, by luck had managed to find him there after a long wait.

Bainbridge was unemployed and the story is best taken up from his point of view, as follows: -

He had bumped into these 'goons', Doug, Danny and Phil at the Miramar Café whilst looking for his girlfriend. This was not an arranged meeting and he was surprised that George Bettis had suggested seeing him over obtaining weapons.

Bainbridge then describes how, on hearing one of them talking about how he was able to get weapons, he was surprised at this and his immediate thoughts were that these were naive men and that he could maybe 'con' them out of a few quid. He falsely suggested that he could probably get shotguns but not automatics and that he would want £25 for expenses. He was bemused as to why George Bettis might suggest that he could. He had no plans to meet them at Kidderminster.

(This was the unbelievable situation which evolved when four absolute romancers who were living in some make-believe dream world where they were all ex-SAS types, who had fatefully assembled together to conspire to appropriate firearms to do a bank robbery, if not to commit a murder.)

Needless to say, Bainbridge hadn't a clue how to obtain weapons and never turned up the next day at Kidderminster.

Latham, McLaughlin, Breakwell, Bettis and Bainbridge, who were more than likely nicely orchestrated by the devious John, and nicely chaperoned by Carol, couldn't have been a more extraordinary mix of idiots involved but whose involvement together, became the eventual unfortunate concoction which caused the death of John Davies.

What actually happened, was that Bainbridge was treated to some drinks at a nearby pub by these Kidderminster boys. Bainbridge, who was supposed to be ex- SAS himself, was told by McLaughlin that Phil was currently in the SAS and that he was merely their chaperon to look after their health in case Bainbridge proved to be a threat. After the Kidderminster trio left him, he had drunk several more drinks and in fact, sold his watch for £1 so that he could consume even more alcohol.

He bumped into a constable in the street telling him in his drunken state that he wanted to report being approached to arrange some guns for a robbery by three strangers from Kidderminster. Not surprisingly, he was moved on and made his own way to Worcester Police Station, where, again in a drunken stupor, found that the desk sergeant also didn't believe his story. He became so irate that he was arrested for breaching the peace when he failed to quieten down.

When sober the following day, he imparted his story to a Detective Sergeant who arranged for George Bettis to be seen by the Kidderminster Police. As a result, the matter was taken no further.

If this didn't involve such a serious finale to John Davies's life, then it would make a comedy which even then, would have been difficult to explain and be treated like anything other than a 'keystone cops' farce.

So now, back to Carol's story as recorded in her statement. The failure to raise the £100 was the cause of the argument at the Council premises, between Danny and her dad. She explained the reason for this as she had in her interviews; her dad was refusing to pay up because Danny had inferred that there would be no payment on getting them on approval. Danny would pay up £50 and her dad the other £50.

Carol recounted that the boys were frightened of George Bettis and that they went to see him to leave him some money so that if the gun supplier, Bainbridge, turned up, he could at least be paid some expenses. They had left their contact numbers so that Bettis could inform them if and when Bainbridge turned up.

Having met up with Danny, Doug and Phil, they discussed their options again at the Bridge Inn. If the guns were to come to fruition as planned, Danny preferred to shoot John and that is what was agreed between all of them, although Carol stated that the others preferred carrying out the robbery. However, because Danny and her dad had fallen out, that was unlikely.

The decision was made to shoot John through his windscreen in the Stourbridge Road, rather than at the rear of the house which might involve Carol's mum finding him.

The time now was 3.17pm on Thursday 29th January and a break for just over an hour was taken so that Carol's solicitors, Mr R. Jones and Mrs. P. Rollason could have a consultation with her.

Unbeknown to them at that time, only a short time previously, at 2pm, the West Midlands Police underwater search unit was searching the canal.

The result of that will follow this chapter, and so, back to the recording of Carol's statement, which resumed at 4.12pm.

She now turned to the time when they were all in the Bridge Inn, but Danny had left earlier. Phil then suggested that they visit the rear of the house to plan an escape and familiarise themselves with the easiest and fastest route out.

[This, of course flies in the face of them shooting John whilst he was driving his van on the Stourbridge Road and the inference here is that as Danny had left them, then their options were still open. Carol, however, was still concerned about her mother being in danger.]

The next important act to be played in this farce was that when they all met at the Bridge Inn on Sunday, 25th. January, Phil declared that he was fixing a light socket and had fallen down the stairs at his home. *[Clearly, Phil had by now, realised that all this shooting of Carol's dad business was a lot more than 'Big Talk'. None of the others, of course, were aware of this story that Phil had contrived.*

George Bettis had not made contact with any of them and therefore, no guns were made available.

It was on the following day, Monday 26th January, that John had resumed his work following his suspension for his alleged drunkenness during his dustcart round. He had, of course, been demoted from being the chargehand driver of his gang to being merely a fellow dustman on another round.

It was when he returned home from work that he told Carol that he had had an argument with a Tony Tupman, who was the new chargehand driver.

Doug and Carol visited the Bridge Inn again at lunchtime. Phil was there but Danny wasn't and nothing about a killing or the weapons was discussed. The same happened in the evening, and again, Danny was absent but again, nothing material to their plans was discussed.

And so, we arrive on the morning of Tuesday, 27th January, the day when John was so violently to meet his maker. Carol's parents had both left for work before they she and Doug later rose at about 10am. She said that Doug lit the fire whilst she did the washing up and then Doug made them a drink whilst she did some hoovering.

She repeated that Doug was fiddling with his watch, but this time, she further explained that he had been trying to get the face clean. They were just getting ready to leave when John came in from work. This would be about 11.15am to 11.30am and after telling John that they were about to keep her dental appointment, they left in her car.

She said that they parked behind Woolworth's and walked to Mr Mike's dental surgery. Her appointment was for mid-day but they arrived at about 11.45am and went to have her surgery at about 12.05pm. She states that the dentist gave her about eight injections and removed eight teeth.

The dental surgeon, Mr. Vernon Mike, provided evidence that at an earlier date, Carol had required all her teeth out because she was emigrating to South Africa in May.

On a previous occasion, he had extracted eight teeth but, on this occasion, he had extracted only seven. The reason for this multi extraction process was because her teeth were going to be replaced by dentures and that there was insufficient time to have her teeth extracted in lesser numbers because there was insufficient time before May, to do it that way.

(What good evidence this was of their intention to emigrate even with them having no funds to do so at that time.)

He was also to say that anaesthetics behave differently on various people, especially if they were taking other drugs. He was therefore not able to comment on her behaviour afterwards.

Carol continued that they left the surgery at about 12.30pm and walked back to the car in which she sat whilst Doug walked through Woolworth's to Edwards's Jewellers to have his watch fixed.

She said that Doug was only away for about a few minutes before returning. She had lain across the seat as she was nearly asleep. After Doug had enquired if she'd rather go home than go for a drink, she opted to go for the drink. They then drove to the Bridge Inn; the time then would be about 12.45pm. Danny was not there but although Phil was present, he didn't join them. Although she had asked Doug for a coke, he bought her a double brandy.

Carol had been sitting at a table in the pub but Doug remained standing. He explained that his chest was still playing him up. She described the people in the bar and nothing unusual occurred. They left the pub at about 2pm and because she was feeling a little 'dopey', Doug drove the car. They discussed Doug's pains and decided that they would go to the hospital that afternoon. She said that when they arrived at the house, John's car was already on the drive and his pick-up was parked outside.

After a conversation about the extraction of her teeth, she asked her dad if he had any change so that they could get petrol to take Doug to the hospital. He gave her £2. She had explained that during the previous day, they had been larking about on the floor and Doug had complained of the pains in his chest. They visited the hospital and he was seen by a doctor who told him to continue taking the distalgesic tablets that he was already taking. If the pains persisted, he was advised to see his GP to arrange for a chest specialist to examine him.

It was after John had given Carol the £2 that he told her that he was 'popping out' later. She asked him if he wanted to borrow her back door key and he said that he would leave it under the mat in case they returned to the house before he did.

Carol said that she would leave him the key and slip the front door bolt off so that it could be opened and that it would be unwise to leave a key under the mat. She said that it was as Doug slipped the bolt from the front door and she was removing the key from her keyring, that her dad stretched out on the sofa and said he was going to have a nap before he went out.

They both left the house by the back door and Carol gave Doug the car keys. Before they left, Doug stood by the back door whilst she put some washing to soak. She said there were underpants, a brown pair, two pairs of blue ones and a white pair. In addition, there were quite a few pairs of socks and some hankies. She ran the water on these items and sprinkled some washing powder over them.

As they drove along Walter Nash Road, Carol said that she asked Doug for 'a fag'. He said, "Ent you got em?" and she replied, "No." She commented that "In the state I was in, I must have put them down in the house." He said "Okay."

They decided between them that they would go back for the cigarettes and as they were passing Meredith Green, they turned right into it and back into Walter Nash Road to the house. Doug got out and went into the house whilst she sat in the car with her chin in her hand. She didn't notice anything and Doug only seemed to be about half a minute. He tapped the window down on her side and passed her the cigarettes through the window.

She continued that Doug then walked around the front of the car carrying in his left hand what seemed to her to be a foot-long piece of mouldy old wood. She said that draped around it was a pair of his blue underpants which looked wet to her. She said that the underpants were between his hand and the object but that she couldn't swear to it. She said that he opened the driver's door and put the object on the floor between the door and the seat.

She then continued with her version of events and said, "What you got them for?" He replied, "Nothing". They then drove off towards the hospital. They stopped at Minster Service Station for fuel and Carol went into the office to pay the £2 while Doug pumped the petrol into the car. As they drew away, Doug said that they had better go and see Danny to see if he was playing darts; by this, she presumed it was the match arranged to be played on the following day at the Bridge pub.

She repeated that she was now feeling sleepy and they drove into Park Lane and turned into some 'scrap' ground, which took them to the canal bridge where they stopped.

She was unsure whether Doug wound the window down or whether he opened the door but whichever, he did not get out of the car. It was then that she said she saw him throw what she presumed to be the blue underpants over the wall and into the canal.

She said that they normally had pop bottles or cans, which they sometimes threw into the canal: either at that place or at another bridge by the swimming baths. She then described the route taken to reach Danny McLaughlin's girlfriend's maisonette, at Grasmere Close It was as they turned into Grasmere Close that Doug said that he felt sick, but nothing else had been said during the journey.

Danny's flat was on the 2nd floor but as Doug reached the stairs at the bottom, she noticed that he threw something soft and white down the rubbish chute. She didn't know what it was, but it had been crumpled up in his hand, something like material.

Danny's girlfriend Lorraine opened the door to them. As they stepped in, Doug asked her if he could use the bathroom, but he didn't say why. She directed him up the stairs.

Danny was wallpapering in the living room and Lorraine said he had been doing it all morning. In addition to those mentioned, Danny and Lorraine's baby was also there, as well as Lorraine's sister, Carol.

Whilst Lorraine made them coffee, Carol asked Danny if he would go up to the bathroom to see if Doug was alright because he felt sick. Danny joined Doug and after 3 or 4 minutes, he returned to his wallpapering. She said that Danny told her that Doug was alright and that he'd be down in a minute.

Doug returned from the bathroom a couple of minutes later and sat on the arm of the chair in which she was sitting. Danny was kneeling down working on his wallpapering. Lorraine and her sister Carol were sitting on the settee with young Sammy, the baby, running around.

Carol said that as Doug was by him, she said something like, "Have you asked him?" She said that by this, she meant had he asked Danny about the darts match? However, whilst they were drinking their coffee, she said that Danny kept looking at her and was grinning. She also said that Doug and Danny were giggling together and that Doug was also grinning at her.

She commented that she didn't know whether Danny was grinning because Doug had told him about the killing or whether it was because of her gums. Whatever, it was at this juncture of writing the statement that a break was taken. (7.25pm to 7.34pm)

It's pertinent to explain here that when Carol made her long and detailed witness statement to the police on the night of the murder, less than two days previously, whilst she included every detail of the visit to Danny's flat, she completely omitted any reference to Doug going upstairs to the bathroom.

Her reference to visiting Danny was that it was just that Doug wanted to ask him about the darts match. It would have been so simple to have contacted him by telephone. Our case included the fact that he wanted to brag about what he had done.

In addition, when McLaughlin was also first interviewed, although he mentioned that he joined Latham in the bathroom, he of course corroborated exactly Carol's story that their visit was simply to talk about the upcoming darts match. No mention was made of the killing of John Davies.

However, McLaughlin later decided to come clean and provide evidence for the prosecution at the trial. His charges of conspiracy to kill had been withdrawn. (More on that later)

In the witness statement he then made, I recorded that when he joined Latham in the bathroom, Latham fully admitted that he had just killed Carol's Dad.

Not only that, but he then told Danny exactly what he ought to tell the police when they would undoubtedly call on him. It was this story which they 'hatched up' together, which McLaughlin had first given to the police.

Importantly, he also recorded in this latter statement that when he returned to the living room, Carol asked him, "Has he told you". He replied that he had.

So, although Carol had volunteered to make this statement, the events unfolded undoubtedly were to prove that whatever Carol was telling us wasn't the whole truth and she was still trying to cover up for her boyfriend.

Where her loyalty lay after her father's death was very important.

So, we now continue with Carol's statement under caution: She said that at between 2.30pm and 2.45pm, they went back to her car, drove to the hospital and parked outside the Casualty Department. Doug went to the reception desk and explained that he had chest pains and that he had been there about the same thing during the previous day.

During the waiting period, they popped outside to have a smoke and Doug went to the loo. During that time, the doctor came out for Doug but he was still in the loo. He had been there for a couple of minutes and on leaving, he went straight into the examination room. Carol then also went to the loo and Doug was being examined for about 15 - 20 minutes.

On leaving the hospital, she drove because Doug was feeling 'bad'. Remarkably, she said that she could not remember whether they called on Phil or not.

Phil of course, had been a fellow conspirator in the killing of John Davies. It is bizarre or unbelievable that she was the driver, yet in such a short time since the murder, she could not then remember whether they called at Phil's house. It was later that she was able to recall that they had not called on Phil.

Was it a coincidence that following John's death, despite Doug feeling ill and going to the hospital, he had previously called on fellow conspirator, Danny McLaughlin and was now wanting to call on the other fellow conspirator, Phil Breakwell?

It would be the prosecution's case that Latham wanted to brag and tell them that the job had been done and no doubt fit his calling at their addresses into his alibi.

However, whilst driving along Walter Nash Road, Doug asked her whether or not she wanted to call on Tom and Sheila's at number 64, which was not far from their home. Tom and Sheila Parry were friends of Doug's and he wanted to inquire if the car they had for sale had been sold.

The only conversation they had otherwise had in the car was about what the doctor had told Doug and that he thought it was a good idea for him to give up smoking, as it irritated his chest.

(When the Parry family were interviewed about this visit, it was learned that Latham would already have been aware that the car he had once been interested in buying some time ago had been sold.

It had been parked outside the house for sale and had not been at that location for some time. It is also pertinent to add that Latham had no money whatsoever at that time, so in any event he would have been unable to buy it.)

As they alighted from Carol's car, they said hello to Wayne and Julie Jagoda, adult brother and sister who had lived at number 1 Clifton Road, four doors away from their home. Carol simply acknowledged them and as this was happening, an ambulance with siren and blue lights overtook them.

This would be at the time they were responding to Betty's emergency call, after she found her husband John's body. As it happened, Tom and Sheila were out, but their young daughter and three sons were there. The daughter made them a coffee and that was when Sheila arrived at the house. They reiterated that they were still interested in the car that had been for sale, but were told that it had been sold.

Having spent about 15 – 20 minutes with them, they left to go home and Carol said that this was at about 4.10pm.

If implicated, they would have known that Carol's mum, Betty would have arrived home and they would undoubtedly have suspected that the ambulance would be attending at their house.

They there saw the police cars and ambulance and a uniformed police officer approached them. This was the conversation she repeated in her statement: -

"As we were getting out of the car, a police officer in uniform came across to us and said, "Caroline?" I said "Yes." He then said, "I'm afraid there's been an accident." I immediately looked at my dad's Rover car, thinking he meant a traffic accident, and it was alright. I then said, "What do you mean, an accident?" He said, "Yes, it's your father."

Doug turned around and said, "Where's Betty?" And the policeman said to me, "your mothers in next door." Doug said, "What do you mean, her dad's had an accident?" The policeman said to me, "I think, Caroline, you'll find he's dead." He then took us both into number 11.

All this of course accords exactly what had been said before. They obviously wished to console Carol's mum, Betty, who was exasperated. It adds nothing to the story to repeat the whole conversation other than to say that in response to attempts to console her, Betty explained that someone had battered John's head in and that his brains were hanging out of his head and there was blood everywhere. She dialled 999 and went outside to meet the ambulance.

At some stage, Carol said that Doug was by a policeman who told him that they wanted the keys to the car, so Carol got them from her pocket and handed them to either Doug or the policeman. Doug was on the front path and told Carol that the policeman wanted him to go to the police station. So, she kissed him goodbye.

She then described their parting by saying, "I kissed him goodbye and as I did so I said, "DID YOU DO IT?" or "Was it you?" I can't remember exactly which." He replied, "No, course I didn't but they'll try and blame us, so watch what you're saying."

Carol explained that she had asked Doug why he had done it, because it crossed her mind that he had done it as he was the last person in the house as far as she was aware.

She then said that she returned to her mum in number 11, to look after her. Her mum said to her after Doug had gone, that whoever killed John had hit him a lot of times because his brains were hanging out. She also said that her mum had told her that it looked as though the fire had been built up and that she had taken three dogs into the shed but not a fourth.

Carol then reiterated in her statement that it was a little later that her mother and herself were taken down to the police station. She was informed by Detective Inspector Herbert and WDC Gwyther that it looked like her dad had been murdered and so they wanted her to describe her movements for that day.

She then recorded in her new statement that what she had said in that first statement wasn't everything because at that time, she was still 'dopey' and half asleep.

She said, "I would just like to add that I didn't kill him. She added, "As far as shooting him goes, I don't really think we would have done it, it was just an idea; I don't think we would really have gone through with it. I don't think I would have had the nerve."

The time was then 8.45pm and a short break of eight minutes was had for the purpose of Mr. Jones consulting with his client, Carol.

The statement continued and she said, "I have spoken to my solicitor about my movements after I drove from the hospital. I don't think I called at Phil's, I'm sure I didn't" She then repeated the directions she had driven in, which would not have taken her in the direction of Phil's.

It will be recalled that, earlier when interviewed, Latham had stated that they called at Phil's house but he wasn't there. Evidence was also obtained from Phil Breakwell's mother that she had been at the house during the material time and that definitely, no-one at all had knocked on her door.

Coupled with the fact that they had made an unusual and needless call on Tom and Sheila Parry's home, the inference here was that they needed to 'pad out' their time before getting home. They would not have wanted to have discovered the body themselves and sadly, contrary to Carol saying earlier that she wanted to protect her mother from seeing John dead, their plan, or at least Doug's plan, was that they should. In addition, a concocted visit to see Phil Breakwell would also be used to fill the time caused by their deviation to the canal bridge.

At the time of making this statement, the details of the burglary committed at Martley had slowly unfolded and when her car had been examined by the police, they found a balaclava mask in it. So, in this new statement, she then turned to that.

She said that Doug had purposely bought the mask at the Army and Navy stores in Kidderminster, in order to carry out this burglary, which he had planned. She said that Danny also had a Balaclava mask and they took a ride out to Martley in the morning in her car to have a look at the place. They were all broke and needed some spending money.

The idea of the burglary at Martley first stemmed from the fact that prior to 1978, John had owned a cottage called Rose Cottage, Shelsley Beauchamp, Martley, in which a tenant, Mrs Jessie Louise Nolan lived. At the time of the burglary, she was 90 years of age. He sold the cottage in October 1978, with the sitting tenant still living there.

It was during discussions about obtaining firearms that Carol disclosed that her father owned a double-barrelled shotgun and that he stored it at the cottage. She further disclosed that her father continued to regularly visit the cottage when Mrs Nolan required maintenance work done to the property. The idea emerged that the cottage could be burgled when Mrs Nolan left the cottage to collect her post.

The trio of Doug, Danny and herself visited the cottage on either 7th or 8th January, about three weeks prior to the murder. Their plan was abandoned however, because Mrs Nolan never left the cottage. They were all short of money and so they decided that they would return later in the evening after dark, to burgle Lilac Cottage, the cottage next to Rose Cottage which was only occupied at weekends.

It was during that night that they returned after dark where Carol stopped at the end of a private road and arranged to pick them up 45 minutes later. She drove around to kill the time and picked them up when she saw a torch being flashed, which was the signal to indicate that they were ready.

She said that they then drove to a car park at the back of the Labour Club where they sorted out their stolen property which they sold at antique dealers in Worcester. This made them a total of £38.

(One wonders if this was enough to cover the expense of purchasing the Balaclava masks to do the job!)

She described the stolen property as two clocks, wooden elephants, a couple of brass candlesticks, a brass dish, three wise monkeys in brass and a couple of pottery pieces which broke and were discarded by them as they were moving away.

The statement then came to an end and as described at the commencement of the summary of it, she signed every page and the caption at the end of it, as did all those present. The time was now, 10.20pm on Thursday 29th January 1981.

It must be remembered of course, that whilst Carol was making this statement, DCI Bullock and myself had left DI Herbert and WDC Jones to plan the next interview with Latham. This would have entailed conferring with DCS Dave Cole and others of the team in the major incident room to gain an appreciation of how the enquiry was progressing.

Obviously, with Carol's statement under caution taking so long to complete, all those other officers involved continued to buzz around Kidderminster, and wouldn't be putting themselves into neutral by sitting around until it had finished.

Many other enquiries continued and we were all very busy indeed, investigating what needed to be done as a result of Det. Chief Superintendent Cole and the Major Incident Room team ploughing through the evidence so far recorded so that they could push out the actions then required to be completed. Someone needed to be the 'ringmaster' and that is why Dave Cole had not got himself involved in any of the interviews.

17. - Douglas Latham – 4th Interview

Being two days into the investigation, there were certainly important actions to be completed. As described in the next chapter, the search of the canal was to be completed imminently and Carol had made her statement under caution. We were now far better equipped to re-interview Douglas Latham and I couldn't wait to see his response to us finding what the witness Mr Millward had brought to the table about their visit to the canal.

I again interviewed Latham with DCI Bullock, and DS Griffiths took the notes. We were in the Detective Inspector's office and the time was 1.15pm. Members of the Underwater Search Unit were about to start their search of the canal. Mr White, Latham's solicitor was present.

The problem with interviewing two suspects almost concurrently, meant that the interview teams involved, might not always be aware of the information emanating from the other team, or what evidence might be forthcoming. In hindsight, I should have waited at least until the canal search had been completed, but I couldn't wait.

We knew of the compelling evidence which the witness Mr Millward, had provided us with, but when we commenced the interview, the underwater search team had not at that time, actually found the wheel brace and the property stolen from the burglary at Martley.

So far as this interview is concerned, I shall try to avoid duplicating the full questions and answers and apart from very relevant material, I will again, summarise the interview where appropriate.

The interview started with me questioning the fact that Latham had stated earlier that Carol and her father were on good terms, yet in interview it transpired that Carol "hated his guts." He denied that she did.

I reminded him that he had previously told us that they had called on Phil Breakwell and I asked him what was discussed. He responded that he didn't speak to Phil because he wasn't there. *The significance here is that evidence existed by now to indicate that they in fact, never even went to Phil's.*

I questioned the fact that he had previously stated that if we found blood on his clothes, then he wouldn't be able to explain it. He said that the dogs were on John and he shooed them off.

I then asked him to go through the meeting with George Bainbridge in Worcester. He explained that it was on the Thursday, the previous week (22nd January) that they went to the address they had been given. They were told that he had moved from there but that he used the Miramar Cafe. They were directed there and sat around drinking coffee and tea for a long time. Danny had been outside and George came up to him and introduced himself. The first thing he said to Danny was, "I could kill you."

On entering the café, George asked them what they wanted and they responded with "**Shotguns and automatic pistols**". Phil was in the café but had not joined the conversation. George said that he might be able to get shotguns but that there was doubt about the pistols.

They then moved on to the pub down the road and Phil followed them a little behind. He said that Phil was just there to "**make sure George was a good boy. I heard he was a bit of a headbanger**".

This statement corroborated evidence at hand in that Doug and Danny were making out to George that their man behind (Phil) was a member of the SAS Regiment and that his presence there was to protect them.

Doug agreed that it was Danny who had approached George Bettis at Sion Hill and that it was he who had put them on to this George Bainbridge.

When asked, Doug said that they wanted the guns for John to do a blag, a bank job. He hadn't mentioned this when first interviewed because, he said, "**I really didn't think of it. I had enough on my mind, I was too busy thinking of who the fuck had done John.**"

I then asked Latham to take us through the argument with Danny at the Council yard. He said that he had seen John that morning and told him that the guns were coming that day. He had agreed prior to anything that when the guns came, he would put the money up.

John then complained that they should have told him about this before he had put the money away, or had spent it. However, that conversation ended by John telling him that the deal was with Danny. Latham then arranged for Danny to see John and they met at the Council Yard.

Phil and Carol were also in the car but it was just Danny who spoke to John. The conversation was heated and a lot of shouting went on, mainly from John about the money and the weapons. Latham explained that after they left, Danny's summary of the conversation was that the weapons were coming, but now John wasn't going to pay for them.

This resulted in Latham stating that he was going to pay anything between £25 to £50 to George Bainbridge for his expenses, but he had no idea how much the weapons were going to cost.

The subject of the bank robbery was then broached and Latham said that originally it was some friends of John's that were going to be involved. It was at a bank in Worcester. When asked by DCI Bullock if he, Carol, Danny and Phil were going to be involved, he said, **"No, not all."**

When pressed what that meant he said that it was John's show and that he didn't want any others except John and himself.

When asked to take us through the plan, he said, **"John said that the bank was in Worcester. It was by a park and it was a Midland Bank. He was going to look at everything around the bank. He was going to find if the bank manager had a wife and children or just a wife. Kidnap wife, children if he had some, park outside the bank with them inside the car."**

He continued, **"Two people to go into the bank, tell the bank manager exactly what happened. Show the bank manager his wife and kids if he had some, ask for the money in the bank and two hours before informing anyone."**

When questioned about those to be involved, Latham said that Danny was only to be involved in getting the guns. He was the only one of the four that would be involved in the robbery with John and John's friends. Danny was going to be involved at a later stage but John didn't like him. When his involvement was discussed, the subject was dropped.

When pressed about his own involvement, contrary to what he had already said, he replied to the DCI's question, "Were you going to be part of this robbery?" He said, **"No, I was not, he wanted me although I wasn't going to be part of it."**

I then asked him why it was that they returned to the house after they had left it to get some petrol.

He responded, **"I don't know what it was that made me go back, that's basically it. I don't know why I went back."**

So far as the route taken, he explained it as previously and it was at this time, 2.15pm that DCI Bullock left the room and returned one minute later. It was now as near as damn it, exactly 48 hours after the murder had taken place.

I cannot remember when or by whom we were informed of the find of a lorry wheel brace in the canal, but as the underwater searcher, PC Golby found it at 2pm, I can only imagine that DCI Bullock's brief exit from the room was as a result of this find and that he had been signalled out of the room to learn about it.

Latham said that the return trip to the house would have taken about a minute: maybe longer, if stopping at road junctions. Carol was in the passenger seat of the Viva and he parked behind John's pick-up truck, 'The Dilly'.

He said that when they had first left, John was half asleep on the settee. When they returned, they parked more towards their neighbour's house in a position where Carol would have seen him walking to and from the house. When asked if he had taken anything into the house with him or if he picked up anything outside the house, he said, **"No, I don't think so, no. I can't really remember. It's a bit hazy, there's no reason why I should."**

Here again, it seems from Latham's point of view, that whenever questions put to him could actually be known by other witnesses and therefore help to incriminate him, he answered with an open-ended answer. His brain here might well have been telling him to be careful in case any of the neighbours, or indeed, Carol could have given information indicating that he did pick up something outside or carry something into the house. By answering as he did, he could always come back and say, "I told you I was hazy and I couldn't remember".

DCI Bullock said, "Tell us exactly what you did and saw from the time you got to the back door on your way in, until you arrived back at the car, having been in?"

He replied, **"Went through the back door, turned into the kitchen, turned into the front room, went towards the mantelpiece er, turned around and saw the dogs around John seen the blood and everything around him, went over, touched his arm. Fucked the dogs off like, and then I think I just turned round and panicked and run out into the kitchen and run into the yard part. Had a look round the back of the house, just panicked and went straight back to the car."**

I said, "Did you go up the stairs at all?"

He said that he didn't and when asked where the telephone was, he said that it was in the hallway. He continued, "Can't even remember if I went into the hallway. It might have been a built-in reaction but I can't remember after I'd seen John, things went kind of blank. Everything goes through your head. It's a horrible experience. You don't know what to do. It scared the shit out of me."

(Again, an open-ended answer)

A four-minute break between 2.33pm and 2.37pm was then taken to allow Latham a toilet break.

When asked, he said that John was dead when he saw him, his head was bashed in. I told him that he must have been aware that he was alive only a matter of minutes earlier. He responded that it was that which scared him so much.

DCI Bullock said, "And therefore might have assumed that by summoning medical assistance, his life may have been saved. You had a telephone in the house which I assume was working. Why didn't you use it to dial 999?"

He replied, **"I never give a thought to anything, all I could see was his head caved in. When you see something like that it drives everything just out of you. I was a blank, I didn't know what to do. I could just see John. I panicked."**

I reminded him that only the previous day, he had said that he was rasping, gargling and he had air in him.

He replied, **"That was one of the things that made me panic more than anything. All I did was touch his arm. It was across him I put my hand on his arm, there was a rasping sound. That was what put the fear of Christ up me. I just don't know what I done I just went I just wanted to get away."**

I then asked him why he went around the back of the house.

He replied, **"I went out because of the sight I'd seen and because of the way I was feeling at the time. I looked around the back because it had been done in the period of time I was away from the house and somebody might have been there still."**

He said that he didn't see anyone at all, nor did he notice any weapon which might have caused the injuries. He also denied that he had taken anything from the house in his hands or his pockets.

I told him that he must have been in a shocked and emotional state, so what did Carol say about his state?

He said that he didn't remember anything until they got to Danny's.

I said, "you're telling me that you were in such a state, yet you were able to walk to your car, drive off and eventually get to Danny's without any conversation between Carol and you as to what you did see. Is that correct?"

He replied, **"Yes, I didn't want Carol to see what I had seen. I remember Carol being out in the car and what it had done to me. Let alone, what it would have done to Carol. "**

I said, "Such a horrible sight. Who do you think was going to discover that sight?"

He replied, **"I didn't. I didn't give it a thought. My only thought was getting away"**.

I told him that he was composed enough to want to shield Carol from seeing the body, yet he would have been fully aware that Carol's mother would discover the body when she returned that afternoon. He questioned that perhaps his composure had failed to account what it might do to her mum.

He replied, **"Carol was with me. She was out in the car waiting I thought of Carol because she was out in the car waiting, I gave no thought at that time, to her mother. One of my deepest regrets now and when I got back home is that I never phoned 999 to save the mother having the sight but at the time, I never thought about it. I just thought about getting away and staying away."**

I said, "Then you drove to the petrol station, did you?"

He replied, **"As I say, I think so, I think I drove to the petrol station, I can't remember from there on in."**

(It was suspected that they may not have gone to the filling station at all, but here again, an open-ended response.)

When questioned about the route he took to get to Danny's, he said, **"I never thought about the route, I don't really remember, all I remember is as I've said before, is getting to Danny's. I don't remember what route I took or nothing."**

I said, "You'd have remembered if you stopped anywhere on route though?"

He replied, **"I don't know if I stopped, I have no recollection. I was thinking too much to stop and start. I just wouldn't have remembered stopping and starting."**

He was then asked to describe what happened when they got to Danny's. He said that as he was feeling a bit off, he asked to use the toilet and he went upstairs to the bathroom.

Carol had said to Danny that he wasn't feeling well and he went upstairs to join him.

He said that he had some blood on his jacket but he didn't know if it was from his hands or the dogs or from where he had touched John. He said there wasn't much blood, just a couple of spots. He said that he wiped his jacket and indicated by his hand his left knee.

When asked if he had cleaned his shoes, he said that he might have done but he didn't think so and he didn't know. *(Open-ended as he wasn't sure what the Forensic Laboratory would find?)*

He also said that he thought that it was a flannel that he used to clean his clothes and that he thought Danny was with him when he was cleaning up but that he was not absolutely sure.

I then asked him what conversation he had with Danny. He replied, **"Er – I turned around and said, I don't know the exact words, John's been done for, I done for him. I hoped there would have been a reaction from this as he might have known somebody who done it."**

DCI Bullock said, "You mean to say that by telling him you done it, you expected him to react in what way?"

He replied, **"He could have said many things. He could have said, "It wasn't you; it was somebody else. He could have said, how, when and why and could have said something that would have let me know who it was that done it."**

I said, "You knew the murder had just taken place and you drove straight to Danny's?"

He replied, **"Yes, I wasn't going at any speed though."**

I said, "How was he going to be able to suggest anybody else?"

He replied, **"I don't know, he might have got somebody else to do it, known somebody who done it. I was just grabbing at anything. I was just trying to find out who and why."**

DCI Bullock then told him that the best way to find out from Danny who had done him was to inform him that he had found John dead and to then ask him if he knew who had done it.

He suggested that telling Danny that he had killed him was statement of fact as opposed to a question.

Latham replied, **"If I had been thinking logically, or like you, was trained to ask people questions, I might have done it that way. I was emotionally unbalanced. I could still see John as he was and that kept going through me mind even when I was talking to Dan. It's a sight you don't forget."**

He explained that Danny knew more people in that sort of world than he did.

At 3.17pm DCI Bullock left the room.

At 3.18pm Mr White left the room at the DCI's request.

They both returned to the room at 3.22pm.

At 3.24pm the DCI left the room with Mr White and returned at 3.26pm to have a cup of tea. The interview re-commenced at 3.27pm.

(The questions that follow appear pointed at the murder weapon and here again, if we hadn't been informed of the wheel brace find in the canal, we most certainly were aware of this at this juncture.)

I said to Latham, "How did you tell Danny that you killed him. What method did you say?"

He replied, **"I just told him that his head was bashed in."**

I said, "Did you tell him what you used to do it?"

He replied, **"Considering I never done it, I couldn't have could I?"**

I said, "But you have told him that you did do it and he must have asked you how you did it?"

He replied, **"No. He just said what happened and I said, he's had his head caved in. I didn't say anything about a weapon or anything like that. Anyway, I can't remember saying anything about a weapon."**

I said, "If it helps your memory, Danny says that you told him that you hit him round the head with what he thought you said, was an iron bar?"

He replied, **"I think that's something he thought I might have said because I don't remember saying anything like that to Danny."**

He then said that he couldn't remember anything else that was said and went downstairs and had a cup of coffee. The young daughter there was playing on his lap and he was tickling her and generally playing with her. He said that he hadn't told anyone other than Danny that he had killed John. He agreed that he had told Danny not to say anything downstairs because of Carol.

I then asked the obvious question in that he had seen Latham wiping blood off his clothes after just killing John and that they had both arrived at Danny's flat. I put it to Latham that surely, he must have asked what part Carol had played in the murder?"

Latham replied, **"He never and I believe that when I was going down I believe that I said Carol didn't know anything about it but there again, that's 50 – 50."**

I said, "Did you take anything into or out of Danny's flat at the time?"

He replied that he had not and in response to a further question, also said that he had not disposed of anything from the time he discovered the body to the time that he arrived at the police station.

In direct answer to the question of him throwing something into the waste chute in the hallway of the flats, Danny denied that he had.

I said "What if Carol said that you did?"

He replied, **"No, I don't recall anything of that."**

I then said, "You mentioned yesterday that you had told people that you were willing to pay £3,000 to anyone who would kill John. Is that correct?

He replied, **"Only two people, yes. Danny and Phil."**

I said, "When was this and under what circumstances?" He replied that he did not recall.

I said, "So, you have told us that you told Danny that you have killed him and that you previously told him that you would pay £3,000 for it to be done and you still insist that you never killed him?"

He replied, **"Yes, I do."**

I said "Why did you wish John dead?"

He replied, **"I did not truly wish John dead as I said before, he was worth more to me alive than dead."**

I said, "Why then, did you offer £3,000 for his death?"

He replied, **"As I said yesterday, it was because John turned around and told me that there was already a price on his head. I was trying to find out who would take such a contract."**

Mr White, Latham's solicitor then interjected and asked, "Did he say why he had a price on his head?" Latham replied, **"No."**

DCI Bullock then said, "So you say when you approached Danny and Phil and told them you were offering £3,000 for John to be killed, you were not, in fact offering this money to kill him, you were only trying to find out on John's behalf, who might have put a price on his head. Is that correct?"

He replied, **"It is in one respect, yes. But I did not at first, offer the job to Phil. I wasn't the first one to approach Phil about it."**

When asked who asked before him, he continued, **"Danny. He was talking to Phil at the Live and Let Live pub at Fernhill Heath. It was after this that Phil got involved."**

I said, "But did he get involved through Danny because you had asked Danny to kill Mr. Davies?"

He replied, **"This, I don't know. You would have to ask Danny. I think it was because of that. It would be pure conjecture on my part if I answered it. That's if I answered it as a straight 'Yes or No."**

DCI Bullock said, "But you do nevertheless agree that you did offer a £3,000 reward for Davies's death, as you've already said?"

He replied, **"Yes."**

DCI Bullock said, "Did you mean them to accept this offer or to kill Davies as a result of the request you were making?"

He replied, **"No."**

I said, "So all you wanted was a reaction from them?"

He replied, **"Not so much from them as Phil is what I consider as way outside. He was abroad and he wouldn't know anybody who would do the bidding as Danny might."**

I said, "At that time, Phil wouldn't even know Mr Davies, would he?"

He replied, **"No, not at that time. I always considered Phil as not able to because of the fact he was going back to Germany."**

I said, "Why ask Phil then?"

He replied, **"As I said, he was involved in it before I had actually spoken to him or that's what I believed."**

I then asked Latham if all he wanted was a reaction about a contract for Davies's killing, then why was it necessary to go into detail as to how and when it would be done?"

He replied, **"The reason for this was to put them off from actually doing it."**

I said, "What detail did you actually go into with them?"

He replied, **"Of how they would actually shoot John and his wife being the thing that would put 99% of people off even thinking about it."**

I said **"But I know you were planning to kill John when his wife wouldn't be present."**

He said, "I don't recall that."

I said, "What were your actual plans?" and he replied, **"I never really had any. Just babblings."**

I then said, "Can you recall a plan, the context of which was that John's wife always went into the house first after a night out and that he stayed outside, fiddling with the car and that's when he could be blasted?"

He replied, **"That's almost right apart from the fact that it was not only him but his wife, which as I said earlier, was to put them off."**

I said, "Did you in fact physically show Danny where he could stand in order that he could position himself correctly?"

He replied, **"Not in so many words, no."** When asked what he meant, he said, **"Danny asked to have a look around the house. Not the inside of it but the gardens. He then said that he could stand round by the shed. I just agreed and said, yes."**

I said "What was Phil's part going to be in this conspiracy?"

He replied, **"Phil was going to be the driver of the car but as I planned about putting them off worked definitely in the case of Phil as he couldn't do it because he supposedly hurt his knee."**

I said, "But you had taken Danny, Phil and Caroline to the area of the house to practise the best means of escape in the car. Didn't you?"

He replied, **"Yes, I did but as I said before, everything I planned to put them off worked. Once he could see that it wasn't a joke. Everything worked as I'd hoped. It put Phil off definitely."**

I said "That doesn't make sense."

He replied. **"You turn round and say to a bloke, you want to kill John. In my opinion, it's something to talk about and it's great as long as it's talking. To really put them off if you show them exactly what it is and get into their brain that it's actually two people, one man and one woman who they are to kill, it makes them think constantly about that and hopefully as in this case, it worked. It scared them off."**

DCI Bullock then said, "Caroline was part of this conspiracy and accepted it was an intention to murder her father. What's more, she says that it was her idea. She says the object was (a) to dispose of her father who she says she despised for his interference and (b) to obtain money from his estate after his death in order to finance you and her going to live in South Africa. It was no joke as far as she was concerned, neither was it chatter."

He replied, **"It was, in my opinion and it was the only way I thought of it."**

DCI Bullock said, "I don't understand all this. You said that you told Danny that you were putting out a contract on the life of John Davies only as a means of finding out who, if anybody, had put out such a contract. Yet you deliberately planned it, you organised it, rehearsed it, discussed it on several occasions, talked of more than one plan and indeed, I understand that plans were hatched between you, to kill John Davies as he drove along the Stourbridge Road whilst taking his metal to the dealers. Do you agree with that plan?"

He replied, **"Yes, and that plan had to be squashed because of the fact that it might have been carried out. Which I did not want to happen."**

DCI Bullock said, "A third plan also came into being I understand, involving Mr Davies being shot at Martley. Did that plan exist?"

He replied, **"Yes, and it had to be squashed for the same reason as the last plan mentioned."**

DCI Bullock said, "I understand that you burgled a house in Martley. That's you, Carol and Danny and stole antiques from there. Is that correct?"

He replied, **"Do I have to answer that? I prefer to talk to my solicitor"**

DCI Bullock said**, "I prefer an answer to the question."**

I then informed him that he could speak to his solicitor, but that we would return to that after he had.

Latham then agreed that he owned the blue Balaclava mask that had been found in Carol's car and when asked why he had it he told DCI Bullock that it was bought to keep his head warm.

DCI Bullock said, "Why was the face altered to form two eye holes then?"

He replied, **"To keep my nose warm."**

DCI Bullock said, "I understand that you are aware of a cottage at Martley in which there is a shotgun and that you had some plans to steal this shotgun for use in connection with the conspiracy we've been talking about. Is that right?"

He replied, **"I'm not sure on the points of law relating to this and I'd like to speak to my solicitor before answering it."**

DCI Bullock said, "You spoke yesterday about financing the purchase of firearms by selling antiques. You said that after killing Mr Davies, you were going to steal some antiques from his house. Do you agree that you said that?"

He replied, **"The question is not right as from yesterday and the answer is 'No'."**

DCI Bullock said, "I understand that you have sold some antiques in Worcester; you and Caroline together. Is that right?"

He replied, **"I take it this is a reference to the antiques stolen from the cottage."**

I said, "What made you say that?"

He replied, "Because one of your questions you said that me, Danny and Carol broke into a cottage and stole antiques."

I said, **"No you are wrong. The question referred to stealing a shotgun."** *It was then agreed by all present that it was indeed, the question prior to that and antiques were mentioned.*

DCI Bullock said, "What I want to say is this. To summarise, as I understand it, all you wanted to do was find out that someone had put a contract out on Mr. Davies?"

"You went into considerable detail in numerous plans involving four people as to how he was going to be killed and then, according to you, you have to make the offence so loathsome so as to deter them from taking part."

"If you really wanted to know whether Danny had put a contract out on Mr Davies, all you had to do was ask him. I suggest to you that like before when you spoke to Danny, that what you said was a statement of fact and not a request for information. You did intend to kill Mr. Davies, it would seem by shooting, but it would appear you couldn't get the weapons."

"Mr Davies was killed and I suggest to you that because your previous plans failed, and because the parties withdrew, that you did it by beating him to death. Have you any comment to make to that?"

He replied, **"Yes, I have. For what you said about the fact that the only reason for Mr Davies not being shot was because of the fact that I or we could not get weapons. I have only just recently purchased a shotgun. If I'd wanted to shoot Mr Davies, it could have been done with this weapon.**

As I did not wish Mr Davies to be dead, I did not use the weapon or allow anyone else to. If I had wanted to kill him, this was a means I could have used. I did not want him dead and I certainly did not, as you have put it, bashed his brains out. I have not killed John Davies."

Mr White, Latham's solicitor said, "Do you know who did?"

He answered, **"No, I do not."**

DCI Bullock said, "Who did you buy the shotgun from?"

He replied, **"A tatter in a pub."**

DCI – "Which pub"

Latham – **"Can't remember."**

DCI – "Where is that shotgun now?"

Latham – **"Stourport Police Station"**

DCI – "When was it taken to Stourport Police Station?"

Latham – **"Can't remember, you'll have to check with them."**

DCI – "Was it prior to Tuesday of this week?"

Latham – **"Yes."**

DCI – "So the shotgun wasn't in your possession on Tuesday, so you had to find alternative means?"

Latham replied, **"If I wanted to kill John, I would have done it when I had the shotgun, but as I've repeatedly said, I didn't want John dead and I wouldn't have bashed his brains in."**

DCI Bullock said, "Who did you buy the shotgun from. Could it have been a man called Steve Morris?"

Latham replied, **"It could have been."**

[It transpired that Latham never bought the shotgun at all. He had borrowed it for a short-term poaching expedition with McLaughlin, during which they were caught and taken to Stourport Police Station.]

DCI Bullock said, "Did you apply for a certificate to purchase a shotgun from the Chief Constable of West Mercia?"

He replied, **"I have an application form. I didn't send it off. You will find the application form on the window of my bedroom at 9 Clifton Road. It was waiting till I could afford the £12."**

DCI Bullock then left the room at 5.06pm and returned at 5.10pm when the interview re-commenced.

I said, "If you knew the identity of someone who had killed John, would you cover up for that person, no matter who it was?"

He replied, **"I don't think I would."**

Mr White, Latham's solicitor said, "Bearing in mind you are facing a murder charge, give a specific answer if you can."

He said that he would not cover up for anyone and, when asked, also said that he wouldn't dispose of any evidence that would assist us.

From the following question, it would then become very apparent that the metal bar had by then, been recovered by the underwater search team.

I said, "On your way between when you left the house and until you were brought to the station, did you drive in Park Lane and stop at a canal bridge?"

He replied, **"As I said before, I can't remember."**

I said, "Did you during that time, throw any article into the canal?"

He replied, **"As I said, I can't recall."**

I said, "From the time you discovered John's body, until the time you were asked to come to the police station, were you over in the vicinity of the canal bridge in Park Lane?"

He replied, **"I don't recall."**

When I asked him if this was because of his state of mind, he replied, **"As I said before, I suppose."**

At 5.17pm DCI Bullock left the room and I said, "Nothing would have upset Carol's mind, would it?"

He replied, **"Apart from her having injections in her arm and teeth, I believe, and feeling groggy, I shouldn't think so."**

I then said, "So if I tell you that she says you stopped your vehicle where I've described and that you put a wrench type spanner into the canal, which was wrapped in your underpants, what would you say to that?"

At 5.20pm, DCI Bullock returned to the office. Latham said, **"What is a wrench type spanner?"**

I said, "Let's clarify the question then – But Latham interrupted and said, **"Anyway, I never threw anything in there because I don't recall the journey, my mind is a blank on that period."**

I then said, "If I also told you that somebody else saw you throw an item into the canal as well as Caroline saying so. What would you say to that?"

He replied, **"As I said before, I do not recall."**

I said, "I'm not asking you to recall, I'm asking you what your reaction would be, having been told that is the case?"

He replied, **"I find it surprising."**

I said, "It wouldn't be surprising if you had murdered John having planned it, carried it out and then disposing of a murder weapon and that all fits from what you have said yourself. You know now that we can prove that you murdered him, don't you?"

He replied, **"No I do not because I didn't."**

I then discussed with him the finding of an axe on the windowsill of his bedroom. He explained that he had purchased it from Thompson and Parkes a few months previously in order to take it to South Africa, as suggested in a book, 'Trans Africa Journey'. He said that he had used it for chopping up different things: wood and animals – rabbits and legs of lamb that John had bought.

Further questions were asked of Latham about this axe but suffice to say here, that after it had been forensically examined, it was ruled out of this investigation. I suppose that at least, it does go towards the undisputed evidence that Latham and Carol were making plans to emigrate to South Africa, despite the fact that they had no funds whatsoever, to fulfil those plans.

I then said to Latham, "Have you in your possession a pair of blue towelling underpants?" Having replied that he thought so, he was asked, where they were now.

He said, **"Either in my room or Carol's I should think. They could be anywhere in the house, they could be downstairs for washing, anywhere."**

He could not remember how many pairs of those he had.

I said, "Doug, let me tell you this; not only were you seen by two persons to throw what could be the murder weapon into the canal, we have recovered it. You did kill him, didn't you?"

He replied, **"No I did not kill him and if we stop here for a year and a half, and you keep on asking me that silly question, I will give that same answer, I did not kill him."**

At the conclusion of the interview, DS Griffiths had Latham sitting immediately to his left whilst he read every question and answer to him. Latham initialled each answer he had given and signed each page of the notes recorded.

DCI Bullock, myself and Mr White left the room just after this procedure commenced and we returned just after the signing up of page 8. Latham then signed a caption at the end of the statement to the effect that he had read the questions and answers as Sergeant Griffiths had read them to him.

The caption was a certification that he had signed every page and initialled each answer, as being a true record of his answers to the questions. Also, that he had given the answers of his own free will and that he had been told that he could correct, alter or add anything he wished.

At the end of this procedure, I offered Mr White the opportunity for his client to make a statement but after consultation with Latham, he advised me that he did not want to make one.

The notes were then signed by myself, DCI Bullock and DS Griffiths and the time was then 7.05pm on 29th January 1981.

Beneath those signatures, Mr. P.J.L. White, Latham's solicitor also signed a caption to say that the 52 pages of questions and answers were put and dictated in his presence, but at that time the notes had not been checked against the notes that he was making himself.

Latham was returned to the cells at 7.10pm.

At 7.29pm I was present in the charge office and accepted the charge against Latham of 'Conspiracy to Murder'. Detective Inspector Herbert charged Latham and after caution, he replied, **"As I said all the way through, I did not kill John Davies."** He was then returned to the cells.

It was then that I photocopied the notes recorded by DS Griffiths and those recorded by Mr White. We exchanged copies of these notes and following our evening meal, I joined up with DCI Bullock and DI Herbert to transfer notes made into our pocket books. This process was continued during the morning of Friday 30th January.

As with most other early mornings, we also held a review / briefing meeting with Det. Chief Superintendent David Cole when the Senior Investigating Officers would join with the HOLMES Major Enquiry system experts to review the process of the actions outstanding and to consider the formation of any further lines of enquiry which, of course, would then be input into the system and allocated.

So before progressing further with other lines of enquiry, this may be a good time to review what happened on the canal towpath: -

18. - Gone Swimming

I can recount many instances during my career when Lady Luck had played her cards to suit my hand. Robert William Millward's little fishing expedition on the banks of the Staffordshire – Worcestershire Canal on 27th January 1981, ranks among the very best of such luck. However, Lady Luck might well have played against me that day. (But she didn't)

I say that, because Mr Millward reported to the police station what he had seen during that late evening of the day following the murder, wednesday 28th January. However, when he was personally thanked it transpired that he had attempted to telephone the 'Major Incident Room' to report what he had seen on two previous occasions. In both, he was told that the Major Incident Room was closed for the day and he was asked to please ring again. No messages were taken and Mr Millward's attempt to report what he had seen was not brought to immediate attention.

His information was the most critical we could have hoped for. It put Latham and Carol at a place which they had not disclosed to us and of course, it led to the discovery of the wheel brace (Murder Weapon). Although one letter of the registration number of the vehicle he recalled was wrong, he had provided us with sufficient evidence to prove that it was Carol's vehicle and that the driver had deposited something in the canal.

What a lesson this was. The telephone would most probably have been answered by a member of support staff, but it might have been a police officer; after 40 years, I honestly can't recall who it was now.

However, you can be assured that he or she would have been given the most suitable advice (and very strongly!} by either Dave Cole or most probably a senior supervisor of the Kidderminster Division.

This was also a lesson for all we senior investigating officers.

Such persons, whoever they were, must be briefed to record all calls received at police stations from people wanting to make contact with any Incident Room, whether manned or otherwise. If not manned, the Senior Investigating Officer must be briefed as soon as practicable afterwards.

I also realised that it shouldn't have been necessary to do this, but very occasionally common sense seems to escape some people. I was once advised by my Sergeant Neville Ovens, whilst we were working at Hereford Police Station, that "common sense isn't so common these days."

I have never forgotten that advice given by him and it was coincidental that whilst writing this chapter, I sadly attended Neville's funeral. He had been a 'wise man' after all, and had retired from the force as the Chief Constable of the Lincolnshire Constabulary.

What a near miss that was, especially when Mr Millward told me later that had he not got through on his third attempt, he would have not bothered to try again.

The discovery of that wheel brace didn't, of course, prove who it was that killed John Davies, but it very importantly pointed the finger at Carol Davies. It suggested that at least, she had been covering up for her boyfriend and at most, she may well have been in the house at the time the murder was committed. The fact that no blood was found on her clothing tended to suggest that she wasn't, though a doubt still lingers.

Anyway, as mentioned earlier, it was just after lunchtime, two days after the murder, on Thursday, 29th January, that members of the West Midlands Police arrived at Caldwell Mill, bridge number 14, to search the location that Mr Millward had indicated to DCI Bullock. This was January and with rubber swimsuits or not and with a silt-lined bottom to the canal, this wasn't going to be a pleasant swim.

At 2pm, PC Golby handed Detective Constable Whitehead the following items, which he had found there in the canal: -

A toolbox, a brass ornament, a green china pot and, most importantly, a metal wheel brace, sometimes referred to as a 'round-headed' spanner.

(These objects were yet to be identified at that time but it was odds on that they would be part of the proceeds from the burglary of the cottage at Martley a week or two prior to the murder and that the spanner might just be the murder weapon.)

Lady Luck had once again placed her hand on my shoulder. Surely it was always the 'good guys' that she favoured?

One will never know how many similar wheel braces were in the canals of the UK at that time, but with it being in the same place, near to other articles which had been stolen during the burglary of the cottage as mentioned above, very nicely increased the chances that these articles and the wheel brace had caused the splash heard by Mr. Millward as he fished.

The metal wheel brace is the type used to undo the nuts on the wheels of heavy goods vehicles. At one end would be the round spanner end which would fit onto the hexagonal wheel nuts. In the other end were two holes immediately opposite each other, into which a small metal bar could be threaded, so as to be able to give purchase to turn the spanner end. In effect, it is a long metal bar adapted for the purpose described.

Lady Luck also ensured that it transpired that John had had two of these wheel braces and that they had both stood upright against some bricks near to the kitchen corner at the rear of the house. They were among many other metal objects and bars which John would have eventually taken to the scrap merchants. However, when this was checked, only one of them remained.

(It might be recalled that Latham stated that, on finding the body, he ran out as fast as he could and had a look at the rear garden. When asked why, he said that the perpetrator might still be there. In such a panic, it would hardly be likely that he would make a search of the rear, as opposed to getting to his vehicle as soon as he could, which was what he had earlier said that he did.

Of course, if Latham had been responsible for the attack on Mr Davies, then he would have needed to have visited the rear of the house to pick up his weapon. This is what is suspected, but of course no evidence was available to prove that.

The point is made however, that if he had been seen to visit the rear garden, he would have required a reason for so doing, which might well be the reason why he volunteered that he went to the rear of the house.)

The spanner found by PC Golby in the canal, together with the other identical spanner found in the location described, was indeed, later shown to Mrs Davies following this discovery. She identified them as being the same as those two spanners which had been in her garden.

The one found in the canal was later examined by both Dr Weston, Forensic Scientist and Dr. Gower, the Home Office Pathologist, who both stated that such an implement could well have caused the wounds they had described in their reports.

Dr Gower described it as a 39cm long wheel brace with a 3cm long shoulder at one end which carried the hexagonal shaped socket designed to fit over wheel nuts. The cross-bar hole being at the other end.

Some of the other objects found in the canal were also identified as having been stolen from the Martley cottage burglary which Latham, Carol and McLaughlin had admitted committing.

19. - The Judicial Process and the D.P.P

Just to emphasise what I have already touched upon earlier, the judicial processes in place at the time of this murder investigation were very different to what they would have been today. We were not then shackled by the Police and Criminal Evidence Act of 1984 (PACE), so at least we had the freedom to detain our suspects whilst we could continue to prove (or disprove) the charges being proffered against them.

Of course, we could not keep them forever without charging them and it was still a tight rope to tread. It wasn't unusual for writs of *'habeas corpus'* to be served on the police on behalf of suspects who had been incarcerated without charge. Such a procedure would be taken on their behalf and on successfully obtaining the decision they desired, they would be either charged or released.

The main reason why such prisoners would not have been charged was because the Judges' Rules then in place dictated that any prisoner charged could not be again questioned by the police about those charges unless the questions were designed to be put where they are necessary for the purpose of preventing or minimising harm or loss to the public or for clearing up an ambiguity in a previous answer or statement.

To overexaggerate an example, a charged terrorist may have admitted making a bomb before he was charged, but, as unlikely as this example would be, maybe someone now ought to ask him exactly where he planted it?? An answer may well result in minimising harm or loss to the public. OR maybe he had told the police that he had planted the bomb in Newport, but after being charged, it couldn't be found so maybe someone ought to ask him to be more specific as to which Newport he had referred? That would clear up an ambiguity.

Before any such questions could be put to the accused, they should be cautioned in the following terms: -

"I wish to put some questions to you about the offence with which you have been charged (or about the offence for which you may be prosecuted).

You are not obliged to answer any of these questions, but if you do the questions and answers will be taken down in writing and may be given in evidence"

Of course, all such questions, answers and the time and place they were put would have to be contemporaneously recorded and signed by those present, as they would after a written statement.

It can therefore be seen why the charging of suspects would be left to the very latest, most convenient time, so that suspects could be questioned after the police were content that their background research had been exploited to the full. In other words, their weapon had been fully loaded and cocked and not just 'half-cocked'.

Another tactic adopted to overcome this problem was that it wasn't unusual for suspects to be charged with lesser offences, leaving the more serious offences open to be subject of further questions which might otherwise have remained outside the scope of the special circumstances as described above.

In this case, the rules concerning the questioning of suspects on charges already having been preferred were still then in operation as they also are, under PACE, so as to protect the rights of suspects.

However, all had admitted being involved in the burglary offence at Martley and although I cannot remember now in what order they were specifically charged with various offences, one will recall that immediately following the last interview with Latham, he was charged with the 'conspiracy to murder' offence. That would serve to keep him in custody, so that further unfettered interviews could be organised about the actual murder, if necessary.

To summarise where we were in our case here, the murder had been discovered during the afternoon of Tuesday, 27th January. It was now 10.45pm, way past bedtime on Thursday 29th January 1981, when DCI Bullock and DI Herbert joined me in the DCI's office to write up the notes of the earlier interview we had completed with Carol Davies.

I booked off duty at 2am on Friday 30th January.

So far as the 'Judicial Processes' are concerned, we mustn't forget that the identification and care of every exhibit, including the body of Mr Davies must be meticulously recorded with an unbroken trail audit so that the evidence, most probably exhibits, can be tracked from one place to another, until it is finally stored or disposed of.

Also, whilst on the subject of Mr. Davies's remains, HM Coroner is required to be informed at the outset and kept informed. To that end, most busy police stations employ coroner's officers who, during those times, were regular police officers. In this case, PC Braithwaite from Kidderminster attended the scene on 27th January and it was he who accompanied the body to the mortuary and later oversaw the identification of it by Mrs Davies's brother.

On behalf of the Coroner for North Worcestershire, Mr Bryan Evers, he would have also arranged for the Inquest to be opened on 10th February 1981. It was adjourned until a later date.

PC Braithwaite also identified the body to Home Office Pathologist, Dr Norman Gower, prior to him performing his post-mortem examination on 27th January. I particularly mention this because it was also on this day, 30th January, that a further post-mortem examination on John was carried out at 5.45pm on behalf of the defence legal teams, by a different pathologist, Dr Thompson. It was PC Braithwaite who also identified the body to him.

In addition to myself and Det. Chief Superintendent Dave Cole, also present were Dr Gower, Carol Davies's solicitors, Mr. R. Jones and Mrs. Rollason and Scenes of Crime Officer, PC Whitehead who would supervise any body part exhibits to be taken from the premises for further forensic examination.

The post- mortem examination was concluded at 7.10pm.

Thankfully, this post-mortem examination occurred during the evening of the 30th January which was also the day when Douglas Latham, Carol Davies and Daniel McLaughlin appeared before a special meeting of Kidderminster Magistrates for the purpose of remanding them in custody. They were remanded until Thursday 5th February 1981 and each Thursday from then on, with no applications for bail being made.

20. - The McLaughlin 'Breakthrough'

It was unbeknown to me that during the evening of Thursday, 29th January 1981, McLaughlin's mother and her partner, Peter Clark, along with his own partner, Lorraine Albutt had all arrived at the Police Station to pay him a visit in the cells.

On the day of the murder, 27th January, he had, of course, been interviewed by DCIs Mayne and Smith after making a short statement amounting to the support of Latham and Carol's alibi. So, it was over the following day, 28th January and during the next day, 29th January, that he had made full confessions of what he actually knew. He was now in custody, having been arrested.

It was now that the barometer of McLaughlin's intended involvement was to register something like the actual truth. We had, unofficially not believed that he and Breakwell would get themselves that involved but we were faced with the dilemma that they had both admitted quite clearly that they had gone along with all the plans which Latham and Carol had put their way. There was no disputing that they had indeed conspired to murder John Davies. However, those plans were so unbelievable, that they both had never believed that they would come to fruition.

So, in McLaughlin's case, he is in his cell and has to be faced by his loved ones, to own up to the lies that he had told and the feeble support with which he had at first attempted to provide Latham. I have no sympathy with him, but he must have been well and truly embarrassed.

It was on the following day, Friday 30th January, that Miss Albutt asked if she could see me. We spoke at 8pm that same evening and immediately afterwards, I spoke to Mrs McLaughlin's boyfriend, Peter Clark. These were very brief interviews and I have no record of what was said, nor can I indeed, remember the interviews. It would be no coincidence though that soon after, I was found in the police club by an on-duty constable who was sent to inform me that McLaughlin wanted to see me in his cell.

From what happened, I can only deduce that Miss Albutt and Mr Clark had wanted to impress upon me that McLaughlin was only joking and bragging about his involvement with Latham and Carol Davies in their bizarre plans. According to her witness statement made later, Lorraine had informed me that she had seen Latham's name on a cell and that Danny had now informed those visitors that it was indeed Latham who had committed the murder and that he had helped him clean the blood marks off his clothes.

It was a little later at 11pm that I was again approached by a uniformed constable and informed that McLaughlin wanted to see me to change something he had previously said. I went to the cells with DCI Poulton and there we had a short conversation with him which was contemporaneously recorded. Whilst he may have been aware that it was Miss Albutt and Mr Clark's intentions to speak to me, he would not have been made aware that they had, in fact, met me.

This was a 35-minute conversation in which McLaughlin explained that he had been taken by police officers out to Martley in connection with the burglary of the cottage there. He said that Doug had said that he wanted a double-barrelled shotgun and not a single-barrel one. He now wanted to add that he thought that Doug was joking and was not serious.

He also mentioned the location of the blood spots on Latham's leather jacket and that Latham had admitted that he wanted to use him as his alibi. When he asked Latham if that was his intention, he told us that Latham responded – "Yes, but don't worry" and he added that he doubted that the police would ever go there anyway. He also quoted Latham as saying, "Don't worry, you've got nothing to worry about at all, if the police do come up, just tell them that we had coffee, talked about the darts match and then left. I think he did then go on about the darts match.

He said he'd been to the pub. He looked at his watch, I think he said it was just gone twenty-five to three, I'm almost sure and he said, "What time did we get here?" I said I didn't know. He said it would be sometime between quarter past and half past."

He explained that during the next day, he went to the pub and told them of the police visit and that as they told the police that they left there at about ten past two, arriving at around a quarter past would fit in. He also mentioned that he should say that they talked about the return match of darts with the Live and Let Live.

He finalised what he wanted to say by saying that the reason why he hadn't taken Doug seriously was because -

> *"Someone who's supposed to have just murdered somebody just don't stand there cool and calm, tell you about a murder and then talk calmly about a game of darts. No one in their right mind would. Even though I saw what looked like blood on his sleeve, I thought he may have had a big fight. Because I've been involved in fights myself and been covered in blood on my coat and trousers."*

McLaughlin then signed the notes as did DCI Poulton and myself. He was informed that I would explain what he had said to his solicitor.

We then returned to the Incident Room, from where I contacted McLaughlin's solicitor, Mr Jones. I informed him of our brief conversation with his client, the substance of which would be that he wanted to tell us the complete truth.

It was on the following day, Saturday, 31st January that together with Policewoman Arthur, I again saw the witness Lorraine Albutt, Danny's partner and the mother of their daughter, Samantha. Lorraine had sought to see me during the previous evening and in fact, had provided a very short statement on the day of the murder just concerned with the short details of Latham and Carol's visit that day. Unbeknown to the officer recording her statement, it became part of their alibi.

As I was aware of these circumstances, Miss Arthur wrote her statement which I guided as to the format and subject area we wanted to be included. Although her boyfriend McLaughlin was still in custody, her statement had, in effect, become a witness statement in support of the prosecution of him, Latham and Carol Davies. It had since become very important to now try and break their alibi and recording these areas would help us to do exactly that.

This second statement therefore contained the following important details which we sought to prove: -

1. Their visit to convey details about Danny's participation in the darts match was completely unnecessary as Danny was already aware of them and Latham knew that.

2. It was Lorraine Albutt's maisonette and she hardly knew Latham and didn't know Carol. although she had seen her once before. She felt uncomfortable in Carol's presence because she was shy and didn't know her. She had met them about six to eight weeks previously, when her boyfriend McLaughlin brought them home from a lunchtime visit at the pub. She had never seen Latham before then and only about two weeks prior to the murder she noticed them fiddling with Latham's car near to her maisonette.

3. When Latham and Carol called at the flat on the day of the murder, Carol asked if Danny was in and when told that he was, she said, *"We was just passing and Doug was feeling sick. We've popped in so Doug can use your toilet."* This, she would have known, was a complete lie because they had already discussed this visit to inform Danny about the darts match.

4. She was able to say that Latham was aware that there was a toilet at the entrance to the flat and that he had never before been upstairs to visit the bathroom. As soon as he entered the flat, he went straight up the stairs and she had tried to persuade him that he could use the downstairs toilet, but he declined saying that he would prefer the bathroom.

   This short conversation was to Latham's back as he had already started to climb the stairs. We now know that there was blood on the front of his jacket and so the indications were that he wouldn't want these to be seen by Lorraine. In addition, he would have known that there was no hand basin in the downstairs toilet.

5. Lorraine had noticed that Carol's teeth had been extracted, in fact Carol told her that she had just had 'NINE' teeth extracted that day. Apart from her gums showing the congealed blooded cavities, she behaved very normally and could not be described as being anything like 'dozey'.

6. Latham later told her that it was seeing blood coming from Carol's mouth after the dental visit that had made him feel sick. She doubted that explanation.

7. Lorraine was able to recall the specific television programmes being aired when they arrived and when they left. These times were later proved by a television scheduler and as a result, the loose times which Latham had discussed with McLaughlin if the police asked, could be tied down to more or less, the exact times. Lorraine indicated that they had both stayed with them for about 45 minutes.

The Director of Public Prosecutions plays their part

Lorraine's visit to the police station to see me was timely because, Included in the processes of justice, it was always necessary in murder and other stipulated serious cases to have a close dialogue with the Director of Public Prosecutions Department (DPP) and his staff. For a start, we required the DPP's consent to proceed to trial on the charges which they would have been consulted about.

Meanwhile, various witness statements, including those of the interviewing officers, were being typed up to eventually form part of the report to be submitted to the Director of Public Prosecutions office in London. It is the DPP's authority which must be obtained for serious charges such as murder to be proceeded with.

And so, with most of the important evidence at hand, on 4th February, 1981, Det. Chief Superintendent Dave Cole, myself and DCI Poulton, met the DPP's representative Mr. Lecke at the DPP's offices.

Apart from a general discussion about how the investigation was progressing, we at Kidderminster had regularly been in discussion about whether or not we believed McLaughlin and Breakwell about their claims that the plans were all 'Big Talk'. Was this just a 'Big Talk' murder that would never be committed, or was it all for real?

This topic may well have been discussed with Mr Lecke but certainly no decision had then been made.

We returned to Worcester later and indeed, I have a note that we went to the Bridge Inn, where most of the conspiracy to murder John Davies was hatched.

We spoke to the licensee and a few customers but so far as I can recall, no evidential values were forthcoming. It was good to get the feel of the place which wasn't far removed from what I had expected. I wouldn't be taking my wife Jo there.

The following day, 5th February, DI Herbert charged Latham with murder. It was remand day for him, Carol Davies and Danny McLaughlin. All three would again appear before the Kidderminster magistrates for another remand in custody for a week.

At 10.50am, I saw McLaughlin in the Charge Office and he said, "I forgot to tell you, one thing the other night. He did say that he hit him on the temple but he wasn't dead. He said that he had to hit him again".

It was obvious what McLaughlin was aiming for and it was then that he asked me directly, if he could give 'Queen's evidence' by telling the truth on oath. Memory and the circumstances to unfold, corroborates the fact that maybe we had not yet then made a decision about him turning 'Queen's evidence'.

Since our meeting with Mr Locke, it would be the DPP's office that was pulling all the strings as to which way we were to turn. My only response to him was, "Do not say anything about this to anyone."

As indicated above, I had certainly been discussing this issue with our boss, Dave Cole and Mr James, our prosecuting solicitor who was by then acting as the DPP's agent.

Dave never suffered fools gladly and with the absence of many smiles as depicted below, he was never enamoured of any villain but you could always count on him to do the right thing as far as the job was concerned. I think we all favoured McLaughlin to be a foolish idiot and a low league thief as opposed to being a murder mastermind but, of course, such a decision would be down to the DPP.

We became unanimous in our belief that no-one could possibly believe that Latham would tout about in a public house, looking for someone to shoot his girlfriend's dad. We were all agreed that they were true in their belief that this was 'bonkers' and that they would make far better witnesses than defendants. This was the view which the DPP agreed with.

And so, both McLaughlin and Breakwell were subsequently seen when they both made 'all-embracing' witness statements which also included verbatim what their previous statements under caution had also said.

In McLaughlin's case, he appeared at Kidderminster Magistrates Court for a weekly remand in custody on 12th February 1981.

As instructed by the DPP, the charge of conspiracy to murder was withdrawn and I immediately took him to the Coroner's Officer's office where, with the help of Det. Inspector Herbert, we commenced to write his statement. We had been formatting his statement from early on that day and although we hadn't finished, I took him to his mother's home at 5pm. There was a need, however, to continue his statement on the following day.

Dave Cole in 1977   **and in 1982**

We needed to hear what his cellmates had been told. Yes, could prison be yet another stage where he could spin his tales of being a hired gun – which, with the charge he was now on remand for, he could well use to assist in authenticating such spin? If that was what he did, it would certainly not do his plea to give evidence for the Queen any good whatsoever.

Peter Herbert and I had already visited Winson Green prison during the previous week, to discover what McLaughlin had been saying.

I shan't name the prisoner but let's call him 'AB'. McLaughlin had joined AB and his cellmate DB in their remand cell. He apparently spent no time in explaining to them that he was on remand for conspiracy to murder.

He told them that after the man Doug had eventually murdered the victim, he called on them and went straight to his bathroom. He said that he had joined him and helped him to locate and wipe away some blood spots.

AB explained that McLaughlin told him that he had at first thought that he had been in a fight because he was so calm about everything. He said that this Doug told him that he hit the chap with an iron bar seventeen times and that "his bird was there watching." Whilst this doesn't prove that she was present, this was the first indication that Carol might well have been there. He later repeated that fact and after being asked, said that he was indeed positive that the killer told him that she was there.

AB could also remember McLaughlin mentioning the alibi and that he wanted a game of darts to be mentioned in it. He also said that he had joined them in talking about the murder but it was just the beer talking and that he had no intention of killing anyone.

In short, this exactly matched McLaughlin's version as to what actually happened. AB also expressed the view that he was 100% sure that what Danny had told him was the truth because he was cracking up since his detention, so much so, that both himself and their cellmate, 'DB' had been encouraging him to ask if he could turn 'Queen's evidence'.

It's important to emphasise here that our visit to Winson Green prison was made before McLaughlin had returned to the prison from court on that day. Both prisoners made very similar statements though DB's mental condition was such that it would never be our intention to use him as a witness. The important point to make was that we had not told these prisoners that he had indeed asked to "turn Queen's evidence."

The three prisoners had been remanded for a further week and were expected to return to court on Thursday 12th February. During the intervening week, it was important that I catch up with reviewing the evidence we had and that I had properly recorded my own evidence. I had to ask myself, "Was there anything we had missed?"

My time in between was taken up with attending Worcester Crown Court in connection with an armed Robbery at the Worcester Post Office Sorting Office. Thankfully, that was adjourned following 'Not Guilty' pleas being entered. This gave me time to spend with the other SIO's to sort through the HOLMES system to ensure that we were making some progress on compiling our evidence in connection with this murder.

Another important facet in the compilation of DPP files, or indeed, any other file for court, is to ensure that the continuity of evidence has been clearly identified. Are all the exhibits properly exhibited in the witness statements? This type of administration is boring work but as silly as it may appear, many cases have been lost in court because such care has not been taken.

McLaughlin had made his feelings known that he wanted to 'turn Queen's evidence'. This, of course, was a subject in debate at that time and at some point, the DPP's office were made aware of it and had agreed.

On 10th February, I called to see Mrs Betty Davies who was then staying with friends in a different part of Kidderminster. It was always good practice to keep in touch with the loved ones of victims, especially under such circumstances. It was, however, a unique experience so far as I was concerned. It wasn't every day that one has their husband killed and that your only child, your daughter, was now in prison on remand, having been charged with his murder.

But I would be lying if I painted this visit as purely a 'welfare' visit. Mrs Davies was going to be a witness for the prosecution against her daughter and I would be treading on glass. We needed to ensure that, as far as she was concerned, we had recorded all the evidence we required. Indeed, it was on this occasion that I managed to record a further witness statement from her. Included in it, among other things, would be her identification of the murder weapon we had found in the canal.

She additionally mentioned the existence of a further brother of John's and she added further details about how she was met by the four dogs when she arrived home to find her dead husband and how the dogs normally react when persons call at the house.

Betty also went into greater detail concerning the relationship as then existed between Carol, Latham and her dad and which, with Carol, had only deteriorated since Latham had moved in with them.

She explained how John had called Latham a 'bad 'un' and that he did not want his daughter to be taken by him to South Africa whether they were married or not. If they had been married, he wouldn't have liked it, but he would not have objected.

Betty was not in fact aware that John had not made a will, but from what he told her, she assumed that he had made one and that he was going to alter it if Carol went to South Africa.

The important fact here, as will be related later, was that John had instilled in both Betty and Carol's minds, albeit falsely, that his will would be favouring Betty to have all of his money and that Carol would receive nothing.

Betty was also then able to provide information as to John's bank accounts which, in total, came to £3,465. So far as their house was concerned, they had only purchased it from the council a year earlier for £9,000. There was a mortgage protection policy of insurance which, on John's death, covered the amount of the mortgage. The house had since been valued at £18,500.

There were also two other insurance policies in force on John's life, but at that stage, their value had not been processed and therefore, Mrs Davies was unaware of the residual amounts they might generate.

In addition, Betty introduced added details about John's scrap metal transactions and his dislike of Danny McLaughlin. In effect, her statement was to include the dotting of all the i's and crossing of the t's, but most importantly, we needed her to identify the wheel brace that we suspected was used as the murder weapon. I showed both wheel braces to her and she had no hesitation in saying that they had been propped up against a pile of bricks near to the corner of her kitchen wall.

She finalised the statement by stating that Latham and Carol had completed all of the administration required to get them to South Africa and for all intents and purposes were still intent on that emigration.

Thursday 12th February was, of course, the day when the three prisoners would again appear at the Kidderminster Magistrates Court. McLaughlin and Latham would have travelled together in the same vehicle from Winson Green prison.

I have no notes about the communications with the DPP's office although as Mr. Michael James, who normally took the Kidderminster prosecutions on behalf of the police, was now acting as the DPP's agent, it would have been he who negotiated on our behalf. However, I would have been fully aware that McLaughlin was about to have his 'Conspiracy to Murder' charge withdrawn and would be a free man that day.

What was going on in his head was something else. I'm sure he hadn't been aware of what had happened since he asked to turn Queen's evidence but during that journey and up until the charge was withdrawn in court, he couldn't have been sure as to what course the proceedings would take. Was he going to be returned on another remand to Winson Green or was he going to start his very long witness statement as a free man? He wasn't sure of what was going to happen. What a lucky man he was about to become.

My memory isn't clear about the actual remand applications in court but unlike Latham and Carol Davies, McLaughlin had not been charged with murder. I'm pretty sure therefore, that he would have been arraigned separately, especially as we knew that his conspiracy to murder charge would be withdrawn. My notes indicate that DI Herbert and myself afterwards, took him straight to the Coroner's Officer's office to commence his statement. We were therefore not in court to witness Latham and Carol being remanded for another week.

21. - The McLaughlin Statement

As previously mentioned, Philip Breakwell was never remanded in custody. We were aware that at this time, he remained in the Army and was at Aldershot Barracks. He would at some time previously, have been notified in writing that his bail had been cancelled and that we would be travelling to see him soon.

For now, however, Breakwell was yet to be seen and here we were at Kidderminster Police Station, about to record the longest statement I had ever been involved in. Although all the worries and tension of whatever McLaughlin had suffered had been brought on all by himself with little help from anyone else. I'm pretty sure he would agree that his foolish behaviour had been responsible for them all.

Here was a 25-year-old man who, already divorced and having brought a young baby into the world, had now fathered another baby and was living with its mother in a council-owned maisonette. Due to his unemployment, he was unable to fully support them. He had been a lorry driver but was now spending his unemployment benefits by visiting the Bridge Inn and other pubs in the area almost every day, playing in their darts teams. As it now appears, he allowed himself to be sucked into planning a murder which he states, he would never have committed.

Nevertheless, he had now put himself in a precarious position. His choice had been to arrive in a Crown Court and serve many years in prison or take his chance by 'telling all'. He was on a fairly sure bet as he had no doubt realised that Latham would be spending many years of his life in prison and would be an old man by the time he was released. Nevertheless, Latham had proved that he could show no mercy to anyone whom he took a dislike to, so for him, it possibly wasn't an easy decision.

One thing was for sure, and that was, that his decision would be critical to how his life was going to pan out before him.

So, immediately after his release from custody, we were sat in an office at Kidderminster Police Station with pen poised and Danny was now to remind himself that on the day of the murder, 27th January, 1981, he had made a witness statement in support of what he knew Latham would have told the police. They had rehearsed what he was to say and Latham had given him his word that all would be well. But it hadn't turned out that way at all.

As planned, no mention had been made of what he had been told by Latham about the killing, no mention of the blood spots they were to clean from Latham's leather jacket and loyal to his word, (if that were possible) he had gone along with everything he was required to say to support Latham's alibi.

During the very next day, DCIs Mayne and Smith were to knock on his door. McLaughlin would have been shaking in his boots; their pathetic plan had misfired and following McLaughlin making a statement under caution, he was charged with conspiring to murder John Davies.

And so, it was at 10.15am on 12th February when this brand-new third statement began. He first summarised the two statements he had already made and this third attempt was to be the icing on the cake. The contents of the second statement he had made under caution were largely true but it being made under caution, he had formatted it as he wished to describe events and the order in which they were made.

He was then shown that statement and he read it through. It was because DI Herbert and myself were then able to format or guide the course of events necessary for him to be treated as a witness, that he suggested in this statement that he could start again right from the very beginning as to how he became involved with Latham and Carol Davies and how he had ended up in court charged with conspiracy to murder.

This was about 41 years ago and my vision is that I chose to write the statement. I am not in possession of the original and whilst it's not that important, it may well have been the case that DI Peter Herbert wrote it; it doesn't really matter.

This statement would commence from much earlier days when both himself and John Davies first made contact with each other, when Danny was first employed by the council as a dustman.

To repeat here, how McLaughlin had more recently become embroiled with Latham and Carol would be pure unnecessary repetition. Suffice to say that Peter and I were at first always suspicious of what he wanted to include in his statement. So far as the defence were concerned, with his track record behind him, he was going to be the perfect 'hostile' or 'adverse' witness during his cross-examination. We had to get it right!

He could obviously be accused of turning Queen's evidence just to get himself off the hook and, of course, any such challenge would be completely true. So, he had to be cautioned that whatever he had to say must be the truth and nothing but the truth even though the true facts might be hard to swallow and would go against him. Now wasn't the time for exaggeration or 'Big Talk' - a role in which he had hitherto excelled.

So, without repeating all the facts that we already knew, it was just the following things that caused our eyebrows to be raised, or even just a smile to appear on our faces: -

1. He thought it was an iron bar that Latham said he had hit John with.

2. At Latham's request, he gave him some toilet paper to wipe away the blood from his shoes. (Blood was indeed, found on the shoes)

3. On returning to the lounge, Latham was definitely asked by Carol, "Has he told you?" There was no doubt that this referred to the murder and not the darts match.

4. Doug had told him that he had been a mercenary in Angola.

5. It was only after their second meeting together (at the Bridge Inn) that Latham and Carol propositioned him to earn some money to kill Carol's father. The emphasis here was that this was said in Carol's presence and hearing. Details about the shooting of him at various locations were described.

6. McLaughlin admitted that the talk about him being on a 'stabbing' charge was completely contrived 'Big Talk' to keep up with their own 'Big Talk'.

7. Subsequent discussions were repeated many times between the three and on one occasion, he asked Carol if she really wanted her own father killed. She replied, "I do, I hate the bastard."

8. Another reason for the killing was that they wanted to go to South Africa where Doug could become a mercenary. It was the money Carol would inherit from John's will which would pay for their emigration and the payment to him for shooting her dad. At that time, Carol was under the impression that her mother would inherit the house and that she (Carol) would receive part of the residue of cash John had in his bank accounts. (Plans to kill her mother were disclosed and made later)

9. Discussions about the killing were held almost every day and sometimes, twice a day at lunchtimes and evenings in the pub. McLaughlin checked with Carol on many of these occasions to ensure that she really did want to go ahead with these plans. He wasn't able to believe it in his own mind. On each occasion, she confirmed her willingness.

10. It was after Christmas time (about three or four weeks before the murder) that he had been convinced that their plans were true because that was when they discussed also killing Carol's mother. Carol had obtained the book on poisons which included death caused by the boiling of rhubarb leaves. This was necessary for Carol to collect the whole of her father's estate.

11. McLaughlin had hitherto not realised that John Davies was the same man that he had worked with as a dustman some time previously. Latham asked him if this made any difference to him shooting him and he answered that it didn't. Indeed, there was already bad blood between the two, as John had once accused him of stealing a cheque book from the council offices where they worked.

12. It was McLaughlin's idea to visit George Bettis in order to obtain weapons with which to shoot John. Latham had stipulated that he wanted two double-barrelled shotguns as opposed to single-barrel, because they would be together to do the shooting. However, Latham changed his mind as he wanted to be part of the alibi with Carol.

13. The visits to the house and behind it were all confirmed with McLaughlin down to every detail of the plan which included the precise location where McLaughlin would stand. Indeed, he had shown DCI Mayne where he was to stand and this was photographed by a police photographer.

14. The visits to Martley were all confirmed but, in addition, McLaughlin confirmed that they had intended to steal the cable previously mentioned by John, which was stored by some 'Tatters' in a field. All details of the burglary and disposal of the stolen items which he also described, were also disclosed. Doug had bought a balaclava mask and he, McLaughlin, had converted an old black football sock for the same purpose. Doug disposed of the stolen property in Worcester and McLaughlin's share was £8.

15. He agreed that plans for himself to travel to South Africa were made due to his false story of being on the 'stabbing' charge. Also, Latham suggested that they could stop in Germany for a while to get some contracts to kill people. He had told him that when doing this mercenary work, he used the name of Brian Ellis.

16. He confirmed their first meeting with Breakwell was when he (Breakwell) was wearing a 'T' shirt with the logo 'DON'T MESS WITH THE SAS' thereon. This had impressed Latham, who chatted him up to become involved in the plan to shoot Davies.

17. Latham had borrowed a single-barrel shotgun and all three were driven by Carol to the countryside on the other side of Stourport. They were caught by the landowner so went out to Martley, near to the cottage which John had owned. Carol went to see her dad's old tenant and the three men went off to take it in turns to shoot the single-bore shotgun that Latham had borrowed. McLaughlin had never shot a shotgun before and this was no doubt some shooting practice for the killing. He then knew for sure that Breakwell had also been enrolled in the plans to murder John.

18. Latham told him that it was a pity that the gun he had borrowed was only a single-barrel gun but anyway, using it wasn't considered because the gun was traceable. (The gun was seized by the police on a later poaching trip to the countryside)

19. Doug had raised John's plan about the bank robbery and that it was because John was then in fear of getting the sack over being drunk on duty, that he wanted to do this 'once and for all' bank robbery. This was fully discussed in Carol's presence.

20. Doug had encouraged Phil to do the murder with McLaughlin, so that Carol and himself could be alibied.

21. He had been approached by John only six days before the murder, to be included in the bank robbery. John had gone through all of the plan with him and had stipulated that Carol was not to be involved. *(This supports the concept that he might well have been setting up Latham and McLaughlin to be taken off the streets for a long time.)* It was then that John Davies asked him if he could get hold of any weapons but he stipulated that he wanted to try out all of the weapons first. (*Another hint that he didn't want to get caught up with the funding or otherwise procuring the weapons*)

22. It was on the next day when they dressed in suits to look the part of 'high class' villains that they went to Worcester to find George Bainbridge and when the 'Fred Karnow's Circus' attempt was performed to try and obtain firearms from him. (*The link between George Bettis and George Bainbridge was never fully bottomed but it was suspected there would be some thread of criminality between the two.*)

23. Doug came up with the suggestion that they could shoot John after the bank job because they would then have the money from the robbery, as well as Carol's inheritance money.

24. Doug had independently taken Phil Breakwell to the house and had showed him the escape route to be taken, which also included making a stop at the canal in which to dump the firearms.

25. Three days prior to the murder, Doug had told McLaughlin that Phil would be doing the driving and that he would be doing the shooting. McLaughlin didn't like this idea because he didn't know Breakwell well enough. However, he was persuaded but then sought Phil out to see if Doug's version was correct. Importantly, it was when Phil said that that was what he understood Doug wanted, that McLaughlin then believed that the whole thing was serious.

Up to that time, he believed that the whole episode was just 'Big Talk.' He recorded that although they might well have thought that he was also serious, that he never had the slightest intention of going through with it and that he knew that as it was getting close to the time, he would have to back out.

26. It was on that night that he learned from Doug that Phil had fallen down the stairs and had been injured and that he wouldn't now be involved. He had seen Phil limping in the pub and he said that he knew in his own mind that Phil had been putting it on to get out of it. That was the last that he saw of any of them until after the murder had been committed. The rest is as transpired as he had indicated in his statement under caution.

27. He had heard his girlfriend Lorraine greet the couple and that she must have directed him to use the toilet downstairs because he heard Latham ask to use the one upstairs. Carol asked him to join Latham to see if he was alright because he had felt sick. It was about five minutes before he had finished applying the first piece of wallpaper, so after washing his hands, he went to see how Latham was.

28. He found Latham with the cold tap running and was holding his leather jacket with his left hand as he was wiping it down with a flannel in his right hand. Latham explained to him that he had just "done her old man in". It was unbelievable what he had heard and his reaction was, "You've what?" He repeated himself and said, "I told you I would have him". He explained how he did it by smashing his head with an iron bar and that "I smashed him on the temple and the bastard wasn't dead so I hit him again seventeen times." He then said, "The fucking blood splattered everywhere."

29. Still not fully having taken this in, McLaughlin said that after questioning him, he explained that he had done it up at the house and that whilst he was explaining this, he remained calm and was smiling as if he was pleased with himself. Latham asked him to look for blood and he indeed found some splashes on his jacket, four or five which Latham wiped off. They were 'spotted' as opposed to being smudges.

30. All the time, McLaughlin doubted the truthfulness of Latham's disclosures and he suspected that he had been involved in a fight. But after expressing his desire that he shouldn't be involved in any alibi, Latham persuaded him that he would be alright if he just told the police that they had arrived to talk about the return darts match with the Live and Let Live public house on the following night and that they arrived sometime between a quarter past and half past two, had coffee and left just after three. McLaughlin continued to doubt Latham and he told him so, to which Latham replied: "Ask her down there."

31. On his return to the living room, Carol was sat alone as the others, Lorraine and her sister, were in the kitchen making coffee. It was then that Carol half whispered to him, "Has he told you?" And she sat there smiling after he replied, "Yes." It was clear to him then that she meant that had he been told that John had been killed. It was when they were leaving that he told them not to send the police to them as neither he nor Lorraine wanted to become involved.

32. Also on leaving, Latham said that they would be going to the hospital which would also add to their alibi. His parting comment was, "Don't worry, we'll see you tomorrow at the darts match." Carol was present and would have heard all of the conversations.

33. McLoughlin felt sure that he had already been told about the darts match by the team captain, Charlie While (Latham was the Vice-captain). Mr While had indeed confirmed that he had personally told all of the players, including McLaughlin, that they would be playing in the match. Also, McLaughlin had never before known Latham to arrive at their flat uninvited and he was sure it was only because of his condition and to involve the visit as part of their alibi.

As stated at the commencement of this interview with McLaughlin, I had never before been involved in the taking of such a long statement. We had started it at 10.15am and at whatever time it was that McLaughlin had first mentioned the poisoning of Mrs Davies by rhubarb leaves, we would have immediately set into train an action to retrieve this alleged book from 9 Clifton Road.

This is where my memory has played tricks on me, because whilst I can vividly remember my disbelief when he first mentioned the rhubarb leaves, I was sure that it was at the very end of the process on the second day of writing the statement. However, looking at the evidence, I realise that it was most definitely during that first day on 12th February, because that is the day that the book was recovered from Clifton Road.

This was a story which fiction writers would have had difficulty in piecing together, there had been so many twists and turns and I can vividly remember him pacing up and down the room while his statement was read back to him at various intervals.

It was during such a period when he was marching up and down in the office, that suddenly, it seemed that just in case, we hadn't been treated to something more unbelievable, he said, "Wait a minute, they were going to kill her mum as well, with rhubarb leaves!"

I almost sighed in disbelief and said something like, "Look Danny, the jury are going to have a hard enough job to believe a half of what you've put in here, let alone another murder by rhubarb leaves! What makes you believe that?" He retorted, "You can prove it. Carol got a book from the library and it's in her living-room now!"

It was Detective Sergeant Alan Digney who, accompanied by Mrs Betty Davies, re-visited the scene at 1.40pm on that day. This, of course, would be the lunchtime period when we broke for refreshments.

There he took possession of a book, 'Dangerous Plants' by John Tampion. At 4pm, the same day, he also visited Kidderminster Library where he showed the book to the Deputy Divisional Librarian, Mr Ronald Hoggarth, who identified the fact that it had been borrowed on Carol's card along with two other books on 12th January 1981.

This book did indeed contain text regarding the veins of rhubarb leaves being poisonous to humans. Furthermore, the traces of the poison could not be detected.

McLaughlin recounted the fact that the conversation about the rhubarb leaves was first mentioned, as far as he was concerned, in the Bridge pub during one lunch-time. He said that it was Carol who raised the subject and that she told him that earlier during that day, she and Doug had gone to the library and borrowed a book on poisons. Carol had explained that it was the veins in the rhubarb leaves that contained the poison.

Although it doesn't make perfect sense, at some point, Doug chipped in and said that her death would be such that it would appear like she had committed suicide.

The end result of the charges preferred against both Carol and Latham, including a charge of conspiring to murder Mrs Davies, will be dealt with in the final chapters of this book. It represented yet another twist in this unbelievable tale.

Anyway, the time was now 5pm and all three of us were ready for a break. We would not be continuing with McLaughlin's statement until the next morning. I therefore took him to his mother's home at 5pm on this day, 12th February 1981.

So, on Friday 13th February 1981, we continued to write McLaughlin's statement from 9.45am to 4.45pm with a half-hour break for lunch. Including such shortened lunch breaks and the odd cup of tea, we had been writing the statement for almost 14 hours in total. I can vividly remember taking him back to his mother's home into what was something like a party atmosphere. He had been a fool and was indeed a very lucky man, even though on that day, it was Friday 13th!

22. - Philip Breakwell's Statements

So, for the first time, after what seemed a long time, Peter Herbert and I took the weekend off. The bad guys were all locked up and the team of evidence gatherers were still gathering evidence although by now, many of the officers who were involved at first would have been stood down, leaving a much smaller nucleus to finish off all of the actions which our HOLMES system had churned out.

As an aside and jumping the gun here, after such lengthy investigations and trials there were always quite large mopping up exercises to endure. I recall that the very last 'action' in the incident room for this case, involved the identification of two suspicious looking characters who had screeched to a halt in their car in a neighbouring street, not far from the murder scene at about the appropriate time.

They had questioned an old lady as to the location of Clifton Road. Indeed, that was where the murder had been committed, so could they somehow be connected? She duly reported this to the incident room.

We eventually identified them as DCI Alan Poulton and myself, who had briefly stopped to enquire where the scene was to be found. Oh well, these things happen! Another action had been completed even though the vehicle in question did not belong to Alan Poulton or myself; ah, but hadn't we been driving that plain police Marina CID vehicle? –Of course!

And so it was that by arrangement, on the Monday, 16th February, Det. Inspector Herbert and I travelled to Aldershot Military Barracks in that same plain British Leyland Marina police car. Philip Breakwell had clearly been right on the periphery of these extraordinary events and although he had been arrested on the day following the murder, he had not been charged with any offence.

He had made a statement which was full and frank, but of course it was a suspect's statement and had to be made under caution. Here again, even though hints as to the topic could be suggested, the statement had to be his and although it was indeed, very frank, it was he who had to format it and not those who were taking the statement.

Although I would have been fully engaged at the time and didn't have anything to do with it, the decision had been made, that Breakwell should be released on Police Bail within the terms of Section 38 of the Magistrates Courts Act of 1952. This is sometimes referred to as 'Pre-Charge' bail and is made at the time when the police would want to make further enquiries into the matter, before charging the suspect.

It must be remembered here, about that which I referred to much earlier concerning the fact that when a suspect is charged, he can only be further questioned to clear up ambiguity or prevent harm or loss to the public at large. Coupled with the desire to dig a little deeper as far as he was concerned, he was also a serving soldier in the Army, so there was little chance of him absconding.

We had now completed the main 'thrust' of the investigation and there was nothing to suspect that Breakwell had been dishonest in the compilation of his statement under caution. There were naturally now areas which he could expand upon and so we similarly sat him down for six hours whilst we compiled his 'once and for all' all-embracing witness statement, with him first including the whole of the content of his statement under caution.

This new 'witness' statement was to comprise of 17 pages and when it came to enlarging on what he had recorded under caution. He certified that he had already been aware that his 'Police Bail' had been cancelled and that he would not be charged with any offence. He quoted that he therefore wished to make his statement without expecting any promise or favour and that he had written it entirely voluntarily.

Without repeating or emphasising the facts already commented upon, the main points he made in his statement are as follows: -

1. He had only known Latham for 15 days including the day of the murder and only recognised Carol as attending the same school.

2. He arrived from Germany on 13th January and had been enrolled into the Bridge pub darts team by the landlord, Alan Lewis, on the 14th.

3. It was at this darts match that he first became involved in conversation with Latham and McLaughlin.

4. He experienced Latham's bragging about being a mercenary on 15th January in the Bridge Inn when, in Carol's presence, he was told by Latham that they were looking for someone to shoot Carol's father. They would pay £1,000 for each of three shots, one in the head, one in the chest and one in the stomach. He did not believe them and thought it to be just 'Big Talk'. A similar conversation took place between the same three on 18th January, again at the pub.

5. On 16th January they went shooting with the single-barrel shotgun at Martley. Breakwell took no part in the burglary but Carol said in the car to Danny so that he would overhear to the effect that, "Does he know he's in the car with a bunch of criminals." He realised that they had been responsible for the burglary. In addition, he also recounted them going to find the pile of copper cable which Carol suggested that her father was planning to steal. It was in an isolated place and Latham suggested it would be a good place to shoot John.

6. On 21st January, he again met Latham and Carol but this time Danny McLaughlin was present. He was invited to join Latham and McLaughlin on a trip to Worcester on the following day. He agreed and was picked up on 22nd January at 10am. Latham was dressed in a suit to play the part of a 'big time' gangster and so they needed to wait while McLaughlin went and also changed into a suit.

7. He had no part to play in any of the negotiations made in Worcester but recalled their search for a man named George. This took them to Northfield Street, Worcester and then to the Miramar Café where they eventually met up with him. He later accompanied them, at a distance, to the Saracen's Head public house.

8. He did not include himself in any of the conversations with George and kept himself away from them. Indeed, it was later learned that George asked who it was that was with them and they chose to make him believe that it was their SAS friend who was making sure that whoever they met would behave themselves.

    It was only during the journey back to Kidderminster that Latham commented that now they knew where they were going to get the 'shooters.' He realised that they needed to meet this George again but once more, although he was now aware that the objective was to get some guns, he had still put all this talk down to just being 'Big Talk'.

9. He mentioned going to see George Bettis on 23rd January with Latham and McLaughlin. Carol had dropped them off in her car. Latham proposed to this George Bettis that the other George (Bainbridge) who they had met at Worcester, would be coming for the weekend and suggested that he could put him up at his house.

    He agreed and although he never accompanied them, they later took some drink to the house, but George Bainbridge never turned up and so they drank the drink.

10. On the same day, 23rd January, he described the visit of all four collaborators when they went to see John Davies at the council refuse tip. He described McLaughlin going to speak to John and when he came back, he told them that he wasn't going to put up the money for the guns.

11. On Saturday 24th January, he was approached in the pub by Latham who told him that he was going to do the shooting and that he could do the driving if he wanted to. He was alone at first but then McLaughlin joined them and he asked if that arrangement was OK.

12. He agreed at first but in the knowledge that he wouldn't be getting involved himself. As far as he was concerned, he didn't believe this was going to happen and this was just 'Big Talk' again.

13. It was during that same evening that Latham asked him if he and Carol could give him a lift home. He agreed but they first drove to Carol's home. Carol was driving and they suggested that he be shown some ways out of the area for when he was driving the 'getaway' car. Carol also pointed out where the barbed wire was and suggested that they went over the garages because in the darkness, they wouldn't be able to see the old and rusty barbed wire.

14. Breakwell had gathered from an earlier conversation that the guns were not yet available but it was because of this planning of the escape route that he now believed the killing was more likely to happen. He went home and devised the plan of falling down the stairs and twisting ligaments in his knee. After telling them that he couldn't drive, he saw them on several occasions but the plan to kill John was never again discussed with him.

The last time that he saw Latham and Carol was on the day of the murder when they left the pub at around 2pm. Carol had had her dental treatment and although her face was swollen a little, she behaved normally.

Summarising his version of events, Breakwell stated that there was no doubt in his mind whatsoever that Caroline was fully involved in the conspiracy to shoot her father. When the proposition was put to him by Latham, at one point, she had been leaning on Latham's shoulder as he was talking about it and although she didn't join into the conversation, she would have heard everything said and was in fact smiling as Latham was putting details of his plans to him.

He had also been told by Carol that her dad was planning a 'bank job'. He recalled that when they made the trip to Worcester, they passed the bank referred to which was one near to the large park (Gheluvelt Park). He was unable to hear much of the conversation, although he did hear Doug mention that it was too risky.

And so, we eventually arrived back in Worcestershire and I had a comparatively early finishing time of 10.30pm. Breakwell's statement was the last of our main witnesses to be finalising. The evidence was all looking good and we could afford to relax a little by comparison with the past few weeks.

23. - Our return to Winson Green Prison

My past experience of taking witness statements from prisoners in custody, to support evidence for the prosecution, is not my favourite subject matter.

The implications are obvious and looking after themselves is, in my view, uppermost in their minds. Specifically, the very good example I have in mind refers to my experience inside Long Lartin maximum security prison. On 10th January 1977 I had been posted as the Detective Chief Inspector (DCI) for the 'D' Division of my West Mercia Constabulary. This was a large (but more rural than most) division, which included the areas of Malvern, Evesham, Pershore and Ledbury. As rural as it might have been, the prison was built near Evesham and was my own responsibility so far as crimes being committed inside it were concerned.

Before my appointment, it had been agreed between the governor of the prison and the Chief Constable that whenever possible, the governor would deal with criminal offences inside the prison by using his own powers to extend sentences etc. However, in cases which involved an investigation, he would contact me and as the head of the CID for the division, I would be the only officer assigned to deal with them. In his words, he wanted me to "treat an investigation here, as you would in any factory outside the prison." In every case, I normally took with me a Detective Sergeant Dennis James from Evesham.

My predecessor took me over to the prison for a meeting with the governor and to familiarise myself with it. In addition to investigations, we were required to constantly exercise our emergency plans concerning incidents at the prison. Besides the Governor, my main contact point in it was the security department. I was soon to learn how much of my time would be spent 'inside'. It certainly impacted to a huge extent on my 'Divisional' work.

Finding witnesses prepared to support a criminal inquiry inside the most secure, 'maximum-security' prison is far from easy, but it was during the following year in 1978 that I found some success.

A notorious gang full of 'lifers' led by the head of 'The Firm' had been bullying a very large black man.

The reasons I had been told were that he was big, black, ugly and thick. Of course, these descriptions had been given to me and were obviously not my own. I'll give him the pseudonym LARGE.

He was in the TV room and had dared to switch the television channel over without asking anyone. He was set upon by a gang of eight prisoners. They broke furniture to assault him with. A leg of a table was used and he was left unconscious with terrible injuries all over. He had suffered a real kicking. At least one of them was never to be released from prison, so being sentenced again would be no deterrent.

My first port of call was to the hospital doctor who told me not to worry about LARGE as his head was, in his words, "Like a blacksmith's anvil". With a statement taken from LARGE, (an accomplishment in itself) the identification of who was in the TV room at the time of the assault was easy and corroborated by prisoner movements being recorded on the security system.

The big surprise; the icing on the cake was that among them I found two Indian (or Pakistani) inmates who between them agreed to provide me with statements. They had been drug-running in Leicester and were quite open (and naïve) inasmuch as they would be expecting some leniency at parole time. Of course, I would be informing the governor that they were helping me, but I made it clear to them that their early release was not in my domain.

The statements were surprisingly, very good and I hotfooted it to the Governor's door because I knew that this would involve prisoner movements. They would not survive if they were to remain in the same prison as these main suspects.

To cut a very long story very short, there were eight suspects but at the end of the day, each had played varying roles. Some, for example, kept watch on the door whilst others were doing the hitting and kicking. Others, of course, including our two drug-runners were just observing. Of these eight, the three main suspects were shipped to different prisons at Bristol, Gartree (Manchester) and Leicester. I couldn't help wondering why the two witnesses had not been moved, but they weren't.

So, on 13th March 1979, following miles of travelling to interview the three moved prisoners, we all appeared at Worcester Crown Court with five of them being charged with wounding Mr Large. Defending counsel had been briefed by a very good Worcester solicitor friend of mine, David Hallmark. I guessed that he, like myself, would have had an idea what would happen.

Large and both complainant witnesses in turn, entered the witness box and refused to give any evidence or even confirm their identities. The case against them all folded and that would be a lesson for me which, whenever we meet, David Hallmark always mentions. I still can't believe that he can rattle off the names of all five defendants. Boooo!

So, returning to Tuesday, 17th February 1981, Peter Herbert and I shot over to Winson Green prison to interview Latham's cellmates, we'll refer to them as HT and SJ. When HT asked Latham why he was on remand he repeated the correct charges and explained that "It was the missus's old man lying on the settee, he had his head caved in." He said that Latham never directly said that he was responsible but never denied that he was.

Through other conversations held with Latham, HT was convinced that he was responsible for the murder but during one conversation he described the victim as having his hands between his knees when he was killed. However, on realising that he might be confessing, he denied that it was him and also stated that there were numerous people who could have killed him, including some enemies from abroad.

HT also spoke of the tales Latham was spinning about being a mercenary and '"killing a load of niggers in Africa." He also said that the deceased was setting up a big bank robbery and that he had threatened to kill Doug if he backed out or had got caught.

He said that his girlfriend would get half of the £80,000 through inheriting from her father and it was that money which would help him escape from prison.

HT spoke of a mate, Danny, turning Queen's evidence but that Latham wasn't concerned as he would be too scared to give evidence. He also spoke of another who was turning Queen's evidence but that he didn't say much about that person. This of course, would be a reference to Phil Breakwell.

So far as JS was concerned, Latham at first told him that he had been remanded for burglary but following JS reading a newspaper report about Latham's remand, he saw that the charge was for 'Conspiracy to Murder', and Latham then admitted that it was true. He said that he had discovered the body which was covered in blood and that there were a lot of people who could have done it.

However, JS later raised the subject again and he asked Latham if he was squeamish at the time, he was killing him. He replied that he wasn't and that he had hit him about twenty times and the victim had 'no head left'. Latham had told him that it was an iron bar and JS presumed it was a poker. Also, Latham had explained to him how the man had tried to defend himself by raising his arm above his head.

JS said that whenever Latham spoke of these things, he would always go back and deny that he was the killer. He finalised his statement by saying there was no doubt in his mind that Latham was the killer and that HT was always in the cell when these things were being discussed.

It's a pity that I have to record here that I'm not sure whether these two prisoners were produced at court. I would be surprised if they had but my uncertainty concerns the fact that it may have been considered unwise to use them in evidence. The doubt in my mind concerns the fact that Latham's story includes the claim that he had not seen the body at all. He and Carol had arrived on the scene after the ambulance and police had arrived. So how would he know about the deceased having his hands between his knees whilst he slept and was assaulted?

The only doubt about that theory concerns the fact that the defence would have been served with all the photographs taken and possibly, Latham may have seen them.

The other reason why I'm unsure whether they gave their evidence or not is because, as frustrating as this always was, police officers interviewing defendants are usually the last witnesses to be called to give their evidence.

Witnesses who have not given their evidence, are not allowed to enter the court whilst everyone else's evidence is being examined and cross-examined.

The reason is pretty obvious. If they were present, then they could so easily be accused of being influenced by what had already been said by other witnesses. In other words, we, especially the police witnesses, couldn't be trusted not to temper their evidence accordingly.

There were indeed, 131 witnesses to be called. I was number 130 and David Cole was the last witness. His evidence was confined to what he did when first arriving at the scene and later, about the continuity of the handling of some exhibits from the post mortem examination and the recovery of property from the canal. But of course, he was kept out of court so that he could not then be accused of relaying the content of what other witnesses were testifying.

In addition, provision was then in place for the defence to accept that some witnesses could be excused attendance and that their statements could be read and accepted in evidence. A good example would be in the case of the first witness which was PC Peter Wilkinson, our police plan drawer. All his evidence would amount to being beyond dispute. He would merely have testified that he had drawn the various sketch plans, which were the ones produced with an exhibit reference number. His statement would undoubtedly have been accepted and read.

So, whilst being sure that giving evidence by video link was not in place in those days, I'm sorry, that after 42 years elapsing, I'm not sure if these two witnesses from Winson Green prison were ever used in person to give their evidence. In any case, it mattered not.

24. - Murder by Rhubarb Leaves

The recording of Danny McLaughlin's mammoth statement over two days heralded what was to be the end of a very busy period and I can recall that I gave myself an extended weekend by taking two additional days off in lieu of those owed to me. It was good to have a four-day break between 19th and 22nd February inclusive.

However, we still had the two suspects, Latham and Carol Davies in custody and charged. They were appearing weekly on remand but the fact that a plan to poison Carol's mother, so as to inherit the complete estate, had emerged and a decision needed to be made as to whether we should charge them with conspiring to murder her, or not.

And so, it was on returning to the police station at Kidderminster on 23rd February that Peter Herbert and myself got together to plan the interviews we were to have with our suspects. When interviewing the prisoners at Winson Green prison, we had not broached the subject of the intended murder of Betty Davies and so, during the following day, we paid them a second visit but no additional evidence was forthcoming.

It was on Thursday 26th February that Latham and Carol were once again, arraigned before the Kidderminster magistrates to be further remanded in custody. So it was on this day that Peter and I interviewed them separately in the cell block interview room, in the presence of their respective solicitors.

We first interviewed Carol Davies with her solicitor Mr Jones. We used a prepared questionnaire and Peter recorded the notes. WPC Jones was also present as we were with a female prisoner. I reminded Carol that she was under caution and told her that we wanted to ask some questions about a plan to kill her mother. There was no response.

Having told her that Latham had already made it known that her mother was to be killed for a particular reason, she responded by saying that, so far as she could remember, he hadn't discussed that with her.

Mr Jones then advised Carol about the caution I had administered to her and she then added, "He said something about it once, I'd like to speak to my solicitor?" This request was, of course, to speak to him in private and in accordance with her rights, this was permitted. Their discussion lasted for about two minutes, following which, the interview resumed. However, Mr Jones told us that he had advised his client not to answer any of the questions about that subject matter.

I then advised both that I would put the questions to her in any event. That I did and indeed, she made no response to any of them. I touched on the alleged plan being discussed, the method to be used and the borrowing of the library book which contained the fact that rhubarb leaves were poisonous. In addition, Danny McLaughlin had already recounted his version of what he knew, as had Philip Breakwell, and the various damning aspects of their evidence was put to her.

Finally, it had to be 'dropped on her toes' that all this evidence pointed to her wishing her mother to be dead so that she could inherit all of her father's estate and not just a small part of it.

In addition to the suggested conspiracy to kill her mother, we had decided that we should again interview her with regard to the murder of her father. She had not then been charged with his murder and so we weren't hindered by the 'Judges' Rules.' We were, however, hindered by Carol's solicitor who again advised her not to answer any of our questions.

As an aside, it is these 'NO COMMENT' interviews that I have only recently written about in another book. I have suggested that the prosecution and therefore, 'Justice' would be better served by making the situation more balanced by allowing juries to be able to take into consideration as to why, if suspects have nothing to hide, these accused persons should be able to simply rely on their right of silence without any inferences as to their guilt.

At present, juries are instructed that such inferences of guilt should not be made merely because an accused person has decided to remain silent, as is their right. So, questions were once again put to Carol which involved us showing her the property recovered from the canal, which included our alleged murder weapon, the wheel brace, and that other property recovered from the burglary at Martley.

If this wasn't a serious matter about the murder of her own father, we might as well have been showing her our holiday snaps as she showed no emotion whatsoever and so, no replies to the questions were uttered at all.

We also asked about her father keeping a shotgun at a cottage in Martley and then I moved on to each of the places they visited after the death of her father, which, of course, we were alleging were all part of an alibi. Importantly, I put it to her that so far as visiting Phil Breakwell's house was concerned, her explanation differed to that of Latham's in that she had said that the visit was indeed made, but Latham said that they did not visit Breakwell's house at all.

Likewise, I put it to her that their visit to Mr and Mrs Parry's home, just around the corner from their own home in Clifton Road, was a ruse just to ensure that they wouldn't arrive home before the body was discovered. There was no reason for Latham to ask if Mr Parry's vehicle had been sold. Latham didn't need a vehicle then and, in any event, he had no money to buy one. Furthermore, according to Mr and Mrs Parry, he would also have been aware that the vehicle had already been sold.

It was my opinion that we were now being shown apparent signs that although the planning of the murder had been made in somewhat shallow 'considered' detail, the committing of it had been more spontaneous than that hoped and planned for. Because of that, they were not as able to consider the details of their 'post murder' alibi in the depth which would have been otherwise desired.

I also spoke of her condition after her visit to the dentists and that she had been exaggerating her subsequent well-being. I put it to her that she had lied about having an injection in her arm and the number of teeth extracted and this was the reason for her blaming her 'dozy' condition for not remembering important facts.

There were other minor issues discussed but after completing the questions, I read them through to her and she signed each page. Mr Jones also signed a certificate at the end, as did D/I Peter Herbert and I.

I was then present whilst D/I Herbert charged Carol with being involved in the conspiracy to murder her mother and also with the murder of her father. She made no reply to either charge and was returned to the cells.

We then went through a very similar procedure with Douglas Latham and our interview with him lasted three minutes, from 10.35am to 10.38am. His solicitor, Mr White was present.

I informed Latham that the purpose of the interview was primarily to put questions to him about a conspiracy to murder Mrs Davies, Carol's mother. I cautioned him after which he informed me that his solicitor had advised him not to make any comment.

I reminded him about what he had already said about carrying out that murder to merely put the other conspirators off. However, I was now able to put further questions to him about those plans, as we now had Danny McLaughlin's witness statement to support the accusation. The hope was, of course, that, with the rationale being that Carol would inherit all of her father's estate if her mother was also dead, it might tempt him into a reaction - but it didn't. He remained silent.

The interview was ultra-short and at the conclusion, Latham and his solicitor signed each page. D/I Herbert, myself and Mr White each signed the certificate at the end of the interview notes.

I was present at 10.44am when Detective Inspector Herbert charged Latham with the Conspiracy to murder Mrs Davies. Following the caution he replied, "I did not conspire to do such." He was returned to the cells.

25. - Mopping Up

The compilation of a file for submission to the Director of Public Prosecutions was an important part of the investigation. It was obviously required to be accurate and easily understood by those having to subsequently read it. They not only included the DPP staff but our briefing solicitor and counsel.

Such files included a general report compiled jointly by the senior investigating officers (SIOs). This included: -

1. Introduction
2. Circumstances leading to offence
3. Charges and suggested charges
4. The detailed movements of prime players
5. Representation
6. Pathology
7. Court appearances
8. Forensics
9. Clerk to Justices and H.M. Coroner
10. Records of interview with suspects
11. Plans and scene description
12. Summary of Evidence
13. Initial activity at the scene
14. Conclusions
15. Antecedent histories of prime players
16. Court Antecedent histories

In this case, the investigators report consisted of 94 pages of A4 paper.

Statements

Statement bundles would need to be prepared with an index of each witness statement in both alphabetical and chronological order.

In our case we prepared nine statement bundles comprising 131 witnesses, many of whom made more than one statement. 798 pages of witness evidence were recorded.

In addition, we submitted two bundles of non-material statements recorded from another 93 witnesses which we regarded as not able to be justified as being material witnesses and hence, not used in the trial. These statements amounted to a further 176 pages.

So far as evidence to be presented by witnesses is concerned, separate bundles describing documents and exhibits are also very necessary. The document bundles would include items such as sketch plans, maps, original notes of interviews etc. The exhibits file would describe all items and documents to be referred to by the witnesses or seized by police. Some, such as photographs, would be in separate bundles. We had three bundles of descriptions of exhibits, amounting to 314 pages. Each one was required to be cross-referenced to the statement page of whoever would refer to each exhibit.

Yes, one alteration or an additional half-page statement inserted would cause all page numbering to be amended. As boring as this procedure was, getting this right was extremely important. Whilst this administration might well be regarded as the 'hard slog' and of course, it certainly wasn't the most exciting aspect of the job, memories of many a convicted person being released due to errors in the administration of the investigation, linger on for ever.   One quickly learns that the compilation of evidence and the proper handling of it are critical to the success of any prosecution. I often wondered if this was the reason for losing my hair!

OK, two prisoners were waiting in custody to be tried for murder, the first hurdle then to be jumped is the processing of them to the magistrates' court so that they become committed - in this case, in custody - to be tried at a later date at a Crown Court.

One of the problems that is never portrayed on TV or film, is that police officers, detectives or otherwise, are never shown as having more than one case at a time to deal with. Readers may believe that these intervening periods of time were adequate to get the cases finalised for the process to court. Wow; what a misconception that is.

I recall in this case that I had been working on a conspiracy to pervert the course of justice involving what was alleged to be a false complaint made by two suspects against two police officers who they said they had witnessed assaulting some prisoners whilst the prisoners were being exchanged from one police vehicle to another. These were so-called respectable school teachers who I had proved were lying about what they allegedly had witnessed. I was also waiting to be called to another Crown Court trial at Birmingham, involving a Liverpool gang who had attempted an armed robbery at the Worcester sorting office.

Things just aren't so straightforward as on TV when the police have investigated heinous crimes, caught the perpetrators and seen them sentenced, all in an hour's screening!

On reflection, although perhaps not felt at the time, the responsibilities carried so as to ensure that all the I's are dotted and the T's crossed, are quite a burden to be carried. I was a main joint author of the 'Investigator's report', but it must be remembered that the majority, if not all of the recording of the witness statements was not made by myself, Peter Herbert or Ian Bullock. We were the interviewers and whilst we were 'heads down' interviewing, other officers were busy scribbling away, recording much of the evidence which would support us.

One of Det. Chief Superintendent Cole's responsibility as the ultimate SIO was to work with the 'Major Incident' team and their HOLMES computer system, to ensure that loose ends were being identified and tied up. There must be a smooth, seamless flow along this road of information flow because one 'pothole' could so easily upset the whole apple cart.

A very good example concerns the evidence gleaned from the landlord of the Bridge Inn, Alan Peter Lewis. He and his wife had only started their tenancy there nine weeks before the murder.

He had dribbled his evidence into five separate statements. His first was made on the day of the murder, 27th January and was obviously taken to describe the comings and goings of Latham and Carol on that fateful day.

Other statements would have been taken as various incidents or events occurred or unfolded as time marched on. These may not have been known about or their significance may not have been attributed to the investigation until later, by which time they would become material and suitable to be used in evidence.

Mr Lewis's fourth statement was taken on 25th February, some 29 days after the murder. I can see that it was primarily made to include his view as to the normal leaving time habits of Carol and Doug, the fact that he had driven Latham to the wholesalers at Worcester by a route which would have passed the bank subject of the so-called robbery in planning and the fact that Danny McLaughlin might have been told about the return darts match to be played on 28th January.

I am now convinced that something casually mentioned independently by both Danny McLaughlin and Phil Breakwell could have been missed. They had both included in their statements that when in company with Latham on Friday 24th January, they were under the impression that Latham wanted the murder to be committed during that weekend – 25th or 26th January.

McLaughlin gave no reason for this assumption but Breakwell added that it had been arranged that Latham and Carol would be playing snooker at the Kidderminster Labour Club (since changed to 'Social Club') with Alan Lewis and his wife Leslie, on that Sunday lunchtime and that it was suggested that he and Carol would thus be alibied.

And so, one can imagine that a statement from Alan Lewis was ordered pretty darn fast. He had, in fact, corroborated the intention to play snooker with them on Sunday 25th January and that this activity did indeed take place on that Sunday. He included that it had been intended to play that snooker during the previous Sunday but that neither he nor his wife were able to attend. The postponed arrangement was then made to play on Sunday 25th January.

That evidence was so vital and emphasises that witness statements should include all background events which may appear not to be significant at the time, but which may later be worth their weight in gold.

And so, it was several weeks before Peter Herbert and I could really relax. In order to properly relax and indeed, in order to be able to catalogue events in proper order, we needed to read through all of the statements whether they were thought material to our case or not.

It wasn't until 4th March that we had finished the first cut of a draft DPP report. From then on, I had been working part-time on my other 'conspiracy to pervert the course of justice' case and also part-time on this DPP file.

Peter and I met again at Bridgnorth Police Station on 26th March to go through it again and knock it into sufficient shape to be able to go and meet the DPP staff. We again travelled to their offices on 7th April.

Our conference with Miss Claire Reggioni and her staff resulted with a requirement to re-visit 10 witnesses to further obtain amended or replacement statements and also to complete and forward the three exhibit bundles and photograph albums. Although we worked on these together for the next two days, I must say that Peter took on the brunt of the work thereafter, which left me able to continue with my other investigations.

It must be remembered that Latham and Carol had not yet appeared at a committal proceeding at Kidderminster Magistrates Court and so, following the completion of this extra work for the DPP, we next met at Kidderminster on 18th May to check through the Committal file for the committal proceeding. Miss Reggioni had stayed the night at the Mount Olympus hotel and so I collected her on 21st May and we went to the Police Station, which includes the court building, for the committal which was conducted satisfactorily.

26. - The Trial

With so many witnesses, it would have been very convenient to have had the trial at Worcester Crown Court but that wasn't to be. In the first instance, our prisoners were arraigned at Stafford Crown Court on 22nd September 1981 purely to hear their pleas and for 'the court' and its officers to hear and make any directions.

For the record, they had both now been identically charged with three charges – 1. Murder of John Davies, 2. Conspiracy to murder him and 3. Conspiracy to murder his wife, Betty Davies. They both pleaded 'Not Guilty' to all charges. When it's thought about, to plead guilty to a conspiracy to murder, in this case, it would have been very difficult not to have pleaded guilty to the actual murder, so 'Not Guilty' pleas were expected all around.

We were subsequently advised that the trial would be transferred to Oxford Crown Court. With all the witnesses to be called, this was going to be a mammoth logistical operation and we were required to provide police minibus transport for all the witnesses who were expected to be called on each particular day. This was subject to a separate operation order, which thankfully, I had nothing to do with.

In hindsight, those arrangements were probably well thought out because we found Oxford not only a long distance to travel, but also the most inhospitable place in which to find a place for us to park. The city council had implemented a new 'Park and Ride' scheme which would be pretty much useless to us with all our exhibits etc to carry. Dave Cole and I had agreed to take it in turn to drive each other to Oxford each day.

I eventually conducted a little conspiracy of my own with a local licensee of a pub quite close to the court. It would cost me a bottle of Scotch but as this was going to be a long trial, I thought it worth the investment. In protecting his car park from shoppers, he had devised a 'one bar' key controlled barrier access. He agreed to my plan, so what could possibly go wrong?

I mention this 'one bar' barrier because, with a key in our possession, on our arrival at this pub, whoever was the passenger, would be required to alight and release the lock on it. It was my turn when I opened the lock and swung the barrier open in what was, the normal routine.

Dave started to drive through the gateway just as the barrier collided with something and rebounded straight into the side of his car causing quite a scrape along the side. The car was fairly new and of course he being a Detective Chief Superintendent and me being his deputy, Detective Superintendent, he was my boss!!! Oh dear!

In those days, having attended evening classes on 'vehicle maintenance' at the local technical college, I was fully into servicing my own cars and I had done a little 'wet and dry' rubbing down and aerosol spraying of the odd scratch on my own vehicles. "No problem" I said, "I'll pop around with my kit and touch it up". During the following weekend, I visited his house to do the job. His car was there but he wasn't, he and his wife were out shopping. I started the job in his absence and eventually, having finished the 'top coat' had rested back in total admiration of a job well done.

It started to rain! No one was in the house to get the car in the garage or otherwise protect it from the rain and I didn't even have an umbrella with me. With the fresh paint starting to combine with the rain and dribble down, oh what a mess! He returned in the meantime and of course, I had to do it all over again. How embarrassed I was!

As mentioned earlier, during the process of any trial, we were unable to go into the court until we had given our evidence. I was listed as one of the last witnesses and was called to the witness box on the 7th day of the trial which was on 19th. November 1981. I was able to use my pocket book to go through the hours of questioning and the cross-examination wasn't too bad. Latham refused to give evidence on his own behalf. That was sensible for him, of course, because he would have been cut to ribbons in cross-examination by our counsel.

It was on the 12th day, 26th November 1981, that His Honour Judge Drake summed up the evidence and the jury retired to consider their verdict. They retired at 10.20am and we hung around until we went for lunch when at 2.55pm the jury returned to give their verdicts. It was this simple process which was to involve the final twist to this remarkable story.

I don't care how strong a case one has for the prosecution; I can guarantee that no senior investigating officer is entirely confident that the jury will bring in the correct verdict. "You never know how the jury will react to what they hear" is a statement made by many well-seasoned detectives over the years.

The foreman of the jury was extremely nervous and could barely be heard. He got utterly confused during the initial stages and as the clerk went through the individual charges on the indictment and at the time when he was expected to announce their verdicts, he turned around with a sense of bewilderment on his face as if to beg help from his fellow jurors.

He gave one verdict which, quite clearly, the rest of the jurors didn't agree with. They muttered and fidgeted and so made gestures towards the judge. The situation became so embarrassing that the Judge directed the jury to again retire so that they could properly sort out the verdicts on each charge. Clearly there were going to be verdicts of both sorts.

The jury duly returned and found Latham guilty to the conspiracy and the murder of John Davies but 'Not Guilty' to the conspiracy to murder Mrs. Davies. So far as Caroline was concerned, they found her not guilty to murdering her father but guilty to conspiring to murder him. The foreman, however, was no more confident than he had been at the first attempt to deliver the verdicts and he delivered their verdict of 'Not Guilty' to conspiracy to murder Mrs. Davies.

If I'm absolutely honest, as I write this 41 years later, I'm still not 100% sure what all of their verdicts were. The fact that Latham was guilty of murder was not in dispute. Even though people who aid, abet, counsel or procure the commission of offences can be tried and convicted of the principal offence, we had expected Caroline to escape being convicted of the actual murder but we thought that in addition to being convicted of the conspiracy to kill her dad, she had an outside chance of being convicted of conspiracy to murder her mother.

We were content, however, that Latham had been potted and the only sentence he could receive was Life Imprisonment.

Caroline was put away for a number of years. I cannot now recollect how many but six years comes to mind.

And so, we brought our car to the front of the Crown Court building so that we could load it up, but we were then approached by the court usher whose duty it was to guard the jury room. He had a serious look on his face. What on earth had gone wrong?

He was so concerned when he told us that he had overheard the jury's deliberations and that they had decided to convict both of the Conspiracy to Murder Mrs. Davies. The Foreman had 'cocked it up' again but of course their guilty verdicts on that charge would have hardly increased the terms of imprisonment that the judge had given them. We thanked the usher and I recall exactly that Dave Cole and I looked at each other and he said, "Come on Humph, let's get home"!

27 – Final Conclusions

So, this drew the final curtain of yet another of those cases which any police officer in my shoes will never forget. I had dealt with other cases which those not involved with the police might regard as 'interesting' or 'exciting'. I was only asked (again) a matter of a few days prior to completing the first draft of this book, how I regarded the authenticity of TV programmes such as 'Line of Duty' and it is such questions which bring home to me a realisation of how people outside the police and judicial system regard them.

My normal response is to impress upon them that such programmes are first and foremost designed in short spaces of time, to entertain. However fictitious they are, I sometimes worry that each one can cloud people's imagination of how our police are regarded. When this is coupled with the bad press of the type experienced in the recent months of 2021 -22, which led to the resignation of the Commissioner of Police for the Metropolitan force, people can so easily have their perceptions wrongly clouded in the worst regard.

I am thankful to fate and those who guided my career for placing me in such a position, but it is only sometimes in hindsight, that the responsibilities of carrying out our police duties are realised. Whether police or not, one realises how easily some have fallen from grace when carrying out such responsibilities and I know I'm not alone when I say that on occasions, the term, 'there but for the grace of God' comes to mind.

If there can be bonuses of being in such places during our vocations, ranking among those that always come to my mind, is the wonderment of how our peoples are moulded in a great big melting pot, not only of all races and creeds, but on the magnitude of differences of character and make-up of each of us, which, of course, moulds us into individuals that we become, in the first place.

It also focuses the mind as to how it is that so many of the people police officers have to meet up with during their tours of duty, have to take advantage of the benefits system.

Here we had the main two characters in this debacle living each day partly off the courtesy of Carol's parents and partly off the benefits system; they abused both to the extent that visiting a public house twice daily, became regarded by them as 'normal'.

There are numerous examples of this type of abuse and how individual we all are. Only recently, (February 2022) I am still suffering the shock of learning how people are demonstrating against being given the inoculations against 'Covid' which could save their lives.

I cannot believe how naive people can be but, at the same time, perhaps it could be me who is the naïve one? Why should I consider that there would never be any objection to this process? 'Has the world gone mad?', I ask myself. Yes, it takes all sorts and we most definitely witness how the other half live.

I only explain these thoughts here at this juncture, because how could it be that some very strongly minded young girl who sometimes displayed a simple philosophy of life, could fall so far under the spell of a 'Mr Walter Mitty' who could influence her to such an extent so as to turn what was a very strong bond between herself and her father, into a monster who would then go to extraordinary lengths to kill him? I could add, a monster who would also plan to kill her mother, but of course, though involved in discussing that subject, whilst the conversations were factual, there was no-one convicted of that deed.

Arthur John Davies's death would never have occurred in the brutal way that it did, if these two people had never come together. That indeed, was their fate and it was the fate of a man, who it must be said, was far from 'clean' living, but who never deserved to die in that way.

Both Carol and Latham have been free again for many years. I believe Latham to be married again and living in the north of England. One hopes that the prison system will have changed attitudes and minds and that he has been rehabilitated. Perhaps it will be age that has finally made him see a little sense – I wonder and I hope that it has, but it was John's wife, Betty who has probably suffered the most and that is where my sympathy lies.

28. - About the Author

Brian Humphreys is now 77 years of age and fully retired. Having retired from the British Police Service in 1994, he became involved as a contractor / consultant in the 'roll-out' of the first computerised fingerprint identification system in England and Wales. This led to him becoming involved in a 'proof of concept' project on this system in the Caribbean Islands at the behest of Interpol and a French software company based near Seattle, Washington State, USA.

After working in that domain for many years, he became a private investigator and developed a Business Association on a Worcestershire Industrial Estate which led to the attraction of funds for its regeneration. He became employed as a police consultant and a member of the West Mercia Constabulary's 'Retired Experienced Personnel' scheme which saw him recalled to assist in the investigation of serious 'cold case' crimes and other criminal investigations. He finally retired as the manager of a challenging school and now continues his genealogical hobbies which have involved him writing other 'social history' books.

His last book, 'The Changing Shapes of UK Policing' concerns his 46 years of involvement with the judicial system in which he describes the changes made over those years and what he calls the imbalance of fairness in the process of criminal investigations which, he alleges, have swung the pendulum of fairness too far in favour of the criminal. He proffers the loss of police contact with communities and the conducting of 'NO COMMENT' interviews as the worst examples.

He continues to have an active life playing golf, table tennis and bowls and keeps half an eye on his four grandchildren, their parents and, of course, his wife, Jo.

Printed in Great Britain
by Amazon

78646445R00115